EMPOWERING PRODUCTIVITY – BOOK 2

℘ USE ℘
YOUR VOICE

The Art
of
Storytelling
with
Dictation

MARY CRAWFORD

Diversity Ink Press
Mary Crawford
www.MaryCrawfordAuthor.com

ISBN: 978-1-945637-56-8
ASIN: B07XVCQPKW

Published September 15, 2019
by
Diversity Ink Press & Mary Crawford
Author may be reached at:
MaryCrawfordAuthor.com

Printed in The United States of America

All brand names and product names used in this book are trademarks, registered trademarks, or trade names of their respective holders. NUANCE® and DRAGON® are registered trademarks of Nuance® Communications, Inc., and are used here with the permission of the trademark owner.

The author or publisher is not associated with any product or vendor in this book. Any opinions expressed are the author's own. Further, Nuance® Communications, Inc. has not endorsed the contents of the book.

To the authors who wrangle words every day
and make magic.

Someday, you'll be somebody's favorite author.

Table of Contents

Table of Figures

Chapter 1 – Introduction: Voice Recognition and Storytelling

Welcome

If you think about it, voice recognition software is the perfect input device for authors. After all, there is a great tradition of oral storytelling. Even though it may seem more complicated, using voice recognition software isn't much different from sitting down and telling your story to a friend.

I can almost see some of you scowling at your computer screen. Many of you have heard dictation is difficult. Some of you may have tried it without success. Hopefully, this book will demystify the process and make it feel like you're chatting with friends in your living room.

After I released The Power of Dictation, many of the follow-up questions were versions of the following: Dictation looks cool, but I'm not sure it's the right tool for me. I can't seem to figure out how to incorporate it into my workflow. My brain just doesn't work that way.

The purpose of this book is to help give concrete tips which will allow you to integrate dictation into your writing process.

Although, I have my own personal writing style, I won't play favorites.

Throughout *Use Your Voice*, the tips I share will be depicted as follows:

 Features tips related directly to dictation.

 General tips designed to help you become a power user of voice recognition software.

 Cautions against potential pitfalls or problems.

 Helpful notes to highlight information.

For our first highlight:

 Tips in this book will be applicable whether you like to plot every single detail or whether you enjoy the freedom of flying by the seat of your pants.

There are several reasons to use voice recognition software. Many authors report their production numbers increase greatly when they dictate. Others dictate to protect their bodies from repetitive stress injuries. Still others, like me, dictate because typing is not an option.

Regardless of your reasons for adopting voice recognition software or your personal writing style, it is my hope that dictation will be the tool you need to soar.

Who am I? – How I Accidently Became an Author

I don't know about you, but when I purchase a nonfiction book purporting to teach me a skill, I want to know a little bit about what makes that person an expert.

In my case, I know a great deal about voice recognition software. Because of my severe cerebral palsy, I started dictating more than thirty years ago. At that time, voice recognition software was considered rehabilitation equipment and a system cost upwards of three thousand dollars.

Fortunately, over the past few years, prices have dropped dramatically, and the technology has improved by leaps and bounds.

I used Dragon® NaturallySpeaking to complete my undergraduate degree and law school. I even used it to take the bar exam. Wait ... What? What are you doing writing books if you're a lawyer?

I'm glad you asked. I have a funny story about that. In February 2002, I developed a migraine which never really went away. After a while, I ran out of sick leave. I tried every possible treatment plan and applied for countless jobs when my health allowed. Unfortunately, the longer I was away from the legal practice, the harder it was to find work.

In February 2009, I discovered my first Kindle. For this diehard reader, it was like a miracle. (My husband who saw how much I spent on books might disagree with this assessment.) I began reading seven hundred books a year. Law school taught me to be a very fast reader. That's great when you're reading case materials — not so great when you need to buy books.

A few years later, I read a phenomenal book by Linda Kage. It featured a secondary character with cerebral palsy. I was so intrigued that I wrote an email to the author asking her if she would consider giving the secondary character her own book. It was my first ever fan letter and I never expected to receive a response. Much to my amazement, Linda contacted me personally. I started beta reading for her. She was a phenomenal cheerleader and suggested that I should venture into writing myself. I was shocked to receive this suggestion since I had always believed I was a terrible writer. My seventh grade English teacher told me I was the worst student he had ever taught. For years, I believed him. Linda encouraged me to explore writing and became my number one cheerleader. Since I was unemployed and completely bored out of my mind, I didn't have much to lose. I started writing *Until the Stars Fall from the Sky* in November 2013.

Of course, back then I didn't know much. So, without hiring an outside editor or having any real plan, I submitted my work to a small publisher. I had heard that people spend years submitting novels for publication, so I wasn't expecting much. To my shock, my manuscript was chosen to be published. My first book was published in June 2014.

Since that time, I have published twenty-four full-length novels, six novellas and three nonfiction books. Linda couldn't know she would create a prolific writing monster. Even though we write to different audiences, Linda has been one of my biggest supporters. I am forever grateful for our friendship. She started me on a career path I never even considered for myself.

That is the story of how a civil rights attorney and disability advocate accidentally became a prolific author.

So, how do I know voice recognition software works to write creatively? I do it every single day. I have cerebral palsy which makes it incredibly difficult for me to type. Voice recognition software and Dragon® specifically has made it possible for me to succeed. I hate to sound like an inspirational meme, but if I can do it, so can you.

My goal is to help you avoid some of the obstacles I've overcome and give you some solid advice to make dictation work for you.

So, Why Are We Here and Other Philosophical Musings

In writing this section, I can't help but remember the advice from my college writing teacher. Tell 'em what you're going to write, deliver on your promise, and tell 'em what you just said.

So, I'm going to share with you my goals and aspirations for this book. More importantly, I'm going to tell you what this book is *not* about.

Before we address what this book isn't, let's talk about my game plan.

First, I'll talk about the basics of voice recognition software. This is just an overview, for more information about getting started, check out my book *The Power of Dictation*. I'll discuss voice recognition software, microphones, computer equipment and helper applications. Transcription and desktop virtualization software (like Parallels and Boot Camp) are hot topics because Nuance® has elected to stop selling and supporting Dragon® Professional Individual 6.0.8 for Mac.

I will also explore helper applications like Krisp and Speech Productivity Pro. Like everything else I recommend (or don't recommend, in some cases), I have no financial stake in these products. I don't receive any income for sharing my opinions.

After we talk about the basics of choosing and setting up your dictating system, I'll discuss some programs commonly used by authors and how they interact with voice recognition software.

Next, we'll delve into the unique challenges of writing creatively while using voice recognition software. I will give some general tips about becoming comfortable with dictation and changing your mindset.

Finally, we will discuss different types of writing styles and how to most effectively integrate dictation into your workflow based on the way you like to write.

Now, let's talk about what this book *isn't*.

I am not a computer geek. I am just an end-user. This is not a programming book. *Use Your Voice* is also not intended to be a comprehensive guide to using Dragon® or other voice recognition software. If you want more information, check out

The Power of Dictation. Most importantly, this is not a book intended to tell you how to write.

I will discuss three common approaches to writing. One is not necessarily better than another. Writing is a very personal thing. What works for me, may not work for you. In fact, what works for me while I'm writing fiction doesn't really work when I write nonfiction. I often adjust my approach to writing based on the final product.

 My goal is not to persuade you to write one way or another but rather give you the tools you need to incorporate dictation into the style which works best for you.

With those caveats, let's start our discussion of dictation basics.

Chapter 2 – The Software Dilemma

If you want to tell your stories using dictation, one of the first dilemmas you'll face is choosing the appropriate software. This decision has become a little more complicated by Nuance®'s decision to pull Dragon® Professional Individual 6.0.8 from the market.

Although, I will discuss several voice recognition programs in the spirit of being thorough, in my estimation if you're serious about dictation, you need to use Dragon® software. Simply put, the other options pale in comparison.

Personally, I own Dragon® Professional Individual 6.0.8 for Mac, Dragon® Professional Individual 15.3 for Windows, and a subscription to Dragon® Anywhere. Although I am currently running Parallels on a 32 GB MacBook Pro with an i9 processor, my go to program is still Dragon® Professional Individual 6.0.8 for Mac. I will discuss why during my presentation of each individual products.

In actual use, the accuracy difference between the Mac and Windows version is negligible. I am able to achieve 97% accuracy with both products. So, your choice boils down to which equipment you own and the continued availability of Dragon® Professional Individual 6.0.8 for Mac from third parties.

Dragon® Professional Individual 15.3

Dragon® Professional Individual 15.3 for Windows is the current version of the original Dragon® product. I have had virtually every edition of this program. I've been using it since before it had numbers.

In recent years, Dragon® has had several versions of Dragon® NaturallySpeaking available. The most common of these is Dragon® NaturallySpeaking 13. However, Nuance® discontinued support of this product in September 2018. If you own this version, it will still work, but it can be slightly glitchy on Windows 10.

The newest version of Dragon® Professional Individual is 15.

After you purchase the product, you need to install updates to bring Dragon® up to 15.3.

This program uses a slightly different speech engine than previous versions. It is extremely accurate out of the box. Additionally, it has a more streamlined transcription function. It even allows you to transcribe files in the background.

There are many benefits to this program. It has great flexibility to account for regional differences in speech and a setting for teenagers. One of my favorite features in Dragon® Professional Individual 15.3 is its ability to seamlessly correct mistakes. Editing is also much easier in the Windows version of Dragon®. You can tell the cursor to move back a specific number of words or up three paragraphs. Additionally, the Windows version keeps a sample of your speech. This is incredibly helpful when you are trying to determine if you made a mistake or if Dragon® misrecognized what you said. The Mac version of Dragon® does not have this feature. As handy as this is, if you are short on hard drive space, you may want to limit how much speech it saves in one setting.

You can also set the sensitivity of the program. At one end of the spectrum is accuracy, on the other end is speed. Since I have computers with quite a bit of RAM, I always leave the setting at most accurate.

Dragon® Professional Individual 15.3 gives you the option of automatically inserting punctuation. Personally, I am not a fan of this feature because I write fiction and sometimes Dragon®'s choices can be wonky. However, many authors have told me they don't feel comfortable dictating all of the punctuation and they like this function. (It can be found under Tools > Auto Formatting.)

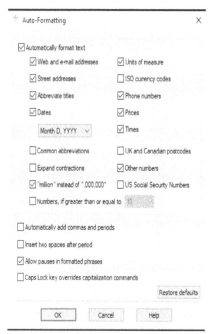

Figure 1: Automatic Corrections Dragon® Professional Individual 15.3

The thing that sets Dragon® Professional Individual 15.3 apart from other speech to text engines is its ability to learn from its mistakes.

It is critically important for you to correct any mistakes resulting from misrecognition.

 Correcting Dragon®'s mistakes is a different process than editing for clarity.

Fortunately, in the Windows version, making corrections is very easy. You select the word and say Correct <misrecognized text> . These days, the program is so accurate that the correct option is likely to be first on the list. If the correct choice does not appear on the list, you simply say Spell That and enter the correct option.

If you have unusual character or location names, you can add them as custom vocabulary words.

Currently, Nuance® offers two versions of speech to text software for Windows. The most basic is Dragon® Home. I do not recommend this product. The home version is stripped of important features such as custom vocabulary and transcription. It is like comparing WordPad to Microsoft Word.

Dragon® Professional Individual 15 is a very powerful program. Unfortunately, this power comes with a steep price tag. If you own a previous version of the software or you are an educator, you can get a discount. Otherwise, the full version typically runs $300. This is one instance in which I recommend purchasing the program directly from

Nuance®. If for some reason dictation doesn't work for you, they have a thirty-day return policy for the Windows version.

Dragon® Professional Individual 6.0.8

So, you have a Mac. Great ... or not.

In a stunning development, on October 22, 2018, Nuance® announced that they would no longer be selling or supporting Dragon® Professional Individual 6.0.8 for Mac.

For Mac fans, this was a dismaying development. Once I got over my shock, I did some investigating, and although it is still an unfortunate development, it is not as bad as I initially feared.

First, despite the reviews you may find on Amazon, in practice, I find Dragon® Professional Individual 6.0.8 to be just as accurate as the Windows version. I'm not sure what accounts for the terrible reviews – other than, in my opinion, Nuance® rolled out the 6.0 upgrade before it was ready for prime time and it was prone to crashing randomly. Subsequently, they have issued several updates. Now, Dragon® Professional Individual 6.0.8 is relatively stable in most situations.

Although Dragon® Professional Individual 6.0.8 is just as accurate as the Windows version, it is not quite as easy to edit documents. There aren't as many navigation commands available and the playback command does not use your actual speech.

You can still transcribe and correct mistakes in transcription to improve the accuracy of your profile.

There are some downsides to the Mac version of Dragon® Professional Individual. Primarily, it can randomly crash. Fortunately, it rarely takes your work with it. Additionally, as I mentioned, it is no longer supported or sold by Nuance®. Therefore, you must purchase it from a third-party such as Amazon, Walmart, Newegg, TigerDirect or Best Buy. At the time I am writing this book, in September 2019, there were copies available at these retailers. I don't know how long their stock will last.

Since Nuance® is no longer selling or supporting this product, you are on your own if you run into difficulties. Support for Dragon® products was never Nuance®'s strong point. So, one might quibble about how strong a deterrent the lack of formal support truly is. Dragon® Professional Individual 6.0.8 is pretty user intuitive. When Nuance®'s decision was first announced, there was some concern about whether Dragon® would continue to work under Mojave and future updates. I can report that, for me, upgrading to the beta version of Catalina caused no difficulties with Dragon® Professional Individual 6.0.8.

Another potential barrier is the cost of Dragon® Professional Individual 6.0. At the moment, it varies greatly. I have seen it as low as $128 and as high as $350. That's a lot to pay for software which cannot be returned.

So, that's a lot of downsides, Mary. Wouldn't you be better off sticking with the Windows version of Dragon® Professional Individual?

Maybe. Except for one program. Scrivener 3 for Mac.

Dragon® Professional Individual 6.0.8 allows me to dictate directly into Scrivener 3.

I don't have to mess around with copying and pasting and I can make full corrections. This is not possible under the Windows version of Dragon®.

The increased functionality of Scrivener 3 for Mac and the ability to work with it directly is enough for me to deal with any minor inconveniences caused by the Mac version of Dragon® Professional Individual. Your mileage may vary and you may value other things more. For me, it was worth the switch to Mac.

Dragon® Anywhere

Dragon® Anywhere is the mobile version of Dragon® Professional Individual. Recent versions of the software have adapted the user interface so it functions more like the traditional desktop Dragon®. However, make no mistake, Dragon® Anywhere is not the same as the full version of Dragon® Professional Individual.

 Even so, Dragon® Anywhere is head and shoulders above the other options available for text-to-speech on phones and tablets.

Depending upon your dictating environment, it is remarkably accurate. Unlike other speech to text engines on the market, you can make corrections and delete your text with your voice. However, there is one important difference between Dragon® Anywhere and the desktop versions of Dragon® Professional Individual. When you make a mistake and choose a word to correct, if the word you wish to use is not on the list, you cannot use a Spell That command to type in the proper choice. You must use the keyboard.

Dragon® Anywhere is not suitable for hands-free use and requires Wi-Fi access to function.

I often use the hotspot on my phone for this purpose.

To be fair, while dictating on an Apple iPhone XR with no external microphone, I had to work extremely hard to encourage the program to make a mistake. It was that spot on.

One of my favorite features of Dragon® Anywhere is the fact that you can customize vocabulary and your vocabulary list is synced across all applications.

When my speech profiles become degraded in Dragon® Professional Individual 6.0.8, I tend to just scrap them and start a new one. Dragon® anywhere makes this process much easier. Dragon® Anywhere can sync with either Evernote or Dropbox. If anyone from Nuance® is listening, it would be phenomenal if Dragon® Anywhere was able to sync with Scrivener or even the mobile version of Microsoft Word.

Personally, I find Dragon® Anywhere frustrating to use because I am so used to Dragon® Professional Individual. The lack of ability to spell corrections by voice is difficult for me. I also think the monthly subscription price of fifteen dollars is a little high, given what is offered. Having said that, after I released *The Power of Dictation*, I heard from several avid fans of Dragon® Anywhere. It seems I may have discounted the value of Dragon® Anywhere for people who love to dictate on the go. Although I still don't recommend this product as your primary dictation tool, it is a solid program and it is far better than the other mobile alternatives. You can try it for a week for free before you purchase a subscription.

Other Speech to Text Engines

There are a few alternatives to Dragon® products. They may be a good option if you want to try dictation before you make a financial commitment. However, keep in mind that these products are nowhere near as accurate or sophisticated as Dragon® software.

On the other hand, most of them are free or can be obtained with a minimal investment. Speech to text software is built into the operating systems on both Mac and Windows. Google Docs introduced Voice Typing a few years ago. Many of the applications which boast speech to text capabilities are based on Google's speech engine.

Mac OS

Rumors that the need for Dragon® for Mac will be obsolete are running hot and heavy since the introduction of the beta version of Catalina. In a blow to wallets everywhere, I am sad to report that the rumors are largely unfounded. Although the demos for Voice Control using the Catalina operating system for Mac are very impressive, during actual use, the program is less impressive.

Mac has included a speech to text engine in their operating system for quite some time. Under Mojave, it works pretty decently. It's compatible with nearly every Mac program. It's easy to access and requires little to no setup. Best of all, it's free. So, what's not to like?

Well, for one thing, it doesn't seem to allow you to train custom vocabulary words. If you write characters with complex, unusual names, or your fiction is set in an obscure fantasy location, the OS speech to text engine is not likely to function well. Additionally, corrections are more difficult to make and the suggestions are not as on-point as they are with Dragon® products.

Finally, there is the issue of accuracy. When testing dictation programs with my Yeti by Blue Mic (one of the best microphones I have ever used for dictation), I was only able to achieve about 84% accuracy with the operating system on the Mac as opposed to 97% accuracy with both Dragon® products. Now, that may not seem like a huge discrepancy, but when you multiply those errors in a one hundred thousand-word manuscript, you begin to see why it's an issue. The 13% difference in accuracy accounts for 13,000 additional errors. That is a lot of unnecessary editing. Free is only free if it doesn't cost you in other areas.

To be fair, I have only evaluated the beta copy of Voice Control in Catalina. The end product could be much more useful. We'll have to wait and see.

Windows 10

For many years, I have watched with bated breath as Microsoft experiments with incorporating speech to text capabilities into the Windows operating system. I'm hopeful each time they introduce a new version because having speech to text capability built into the operating system would increase accessibility astronomically.

When Microsoft announced they were introducing a speech to text engine that was based on Cortana, I was ecstatic. I figured this was the best chance to make dreams reality. You may think I'm joking, but over the past thirty years, I have spent thousands of dollars on dictation equipment and software. I would love for there to be a viable free alternative. Unfortunately, the speech to text engine in Windows 10 is not the program of my dreams.

In head-to-head testing with Dragon® Professional Individual 15.3, Dragon® Professional Individual 6.0.8, and the speech to text engine in the Mac OS, the Windows OS came in a dismal third with only 67% accuracy. Put simply, that's one out of every three words wrong. If you are serious about dictation, the Windows operating system is not the solution for you. Additionally, there is no mechanism for custom words or learning from your mistakes.

The best thing I can say about the speech to text engine in Microsoft Windows is that it is free. If you want to test out dictation to see if it will work for you, you can try to use the built-in speech to text capabilities in Windows 10. Beyond that, the program is not suitable for heavy dictation loads.

Google Docs

A couple of years ago, Google Docs incorporated dictation capabilities into their suite of programs. This free service is actually fairly accurate and if it were complete, it would be phenomenal. Unfortunately, the desktop version is missing key components authors need. You know ... like basic punctuation. I'm not talking about exotic punctuation like tildes or ampersands, I'm referring to basic things like quotation marks, colons and semicolons. Additionally, you can't make corrections by voice. One of the most annoying limitations is its tendency to timeout after a couple of paragraphs of dictation. These deficits have a negative effect on productivity.

If you are using the Google Docs application on your iPhone or iPad, the experience is slightly different.

There is an interesting limitation to using Google Docs. Apparently, you can't use cuss words on the desktop version. They will appear in your document like this: s*** or f***. There don't seem to be any of those limitations on the IOS version. For some of you who don't write clean and wholesome works, the censoring may present a problem.

Since I highlighted these deficits in *The Power of Dictation*, I have heard from several diehard fans of Google Docs. Many of them are willing to go back and edit punctuation into their documents for the freedom of being able to have a web-based program which allows them to collaborate with other people.

If you want the freedom of having access to your documents wherever you have Wi-Fi access and collaborating with other people is important to you, Google Docs may be just the ticket. Just be aware the program has high accuracy, but lacks basic amenities — which I find indispensable. As always, it is up to you to weigh what is most important.

Speech Notes

SpeechNotes is a handy little extension for your chrome browser. It allows you to save the dictation as a .TXT or a .DOC. Additionally, you can upload your dictation to Google Docs. There is an Android version of this program as well. The user interface is clean and uncluttered. The program is free, however the premium mode (lifetime access for $10) allows you to dictate in dark mode. As a migraine sufferer, this is a feature I really appreciate.

The accuracy is spot on and unlike Google Docs, this application allows you to dictate a full complement of punctuation.

This would be a great application except for one small oversight. You can't make corrections to your dictation by voice. This is a major deterrent for me.

If your writing vocabulary includes cuss words, you will be subject to the same limitations as under the desktop version of Google Docs. Words will appear censored.

Now that you've been brought up to speed on your software options, it is time to contemplate the best way to make your dictation software understand what you say. Let's explore the world of microphones.

Chapter 3 – The Vast World of Microphones

Thanks to the popularity of podcasts and home recording, the variety of microphones has exploded in recent years. In the past, high quality microphones were sold in specialty stores and represented a huge investment. Now, you can get a better than decent mic for less than fifty dollars.

My husband likes to tease me about the box in the garage which serves as my graveyard for old microphones. I have a difficult time throwing them away (even if they don't work particularly well). In my thirty years of using voice recognition software, I have accumulated quite a collection. Some of my mics are cheap mics from big-box stores, others are microphones specifically developed for use with voice recognition software.

Ironically, the microphones supplied by Dragon® are among the worst. You would think that if Dragon® went to the effort of packaging a microphone with its program, it would be a time tested, vetted, top-of-the-line microphone. This is simply not the case.

So, if you have the option to purchase Dragon® packaged with a microphone, don't bother. If you buy it separately, you'll have a larger selection.

Basically, there are four types of microphones. Desktop, headsets, lapel mics (also known as lavalier microphones), and wireless. Which one you choose depends on how you plan to dictate.

I have recently discovered another exciting alternative. Krisp changes the landscape of microphone technology in a way I've never seen before.

Regardless of what type of microphone you choose, it is a good idea to choose one with a cardioid model which has a separate gain setting.

Desktop

I am pretty much bed bound. So, I don't move around much. Desktop microphones are perfect for me. They don't interfere with my glasses and I don't have to have them right in my face.

Without exception, the best microphone I have ever used is the Yeti by Blue Mic. I love this thing!

Figure 2: Yeti Microphone with Fuzzy Cover

This desktop microphone has a cardioid setting and separate gain control. If you want to use it for podcasts, music or other applications, it has a variety of microphone settings, including omnidirectional and bidirectional. Simply put, it is a workhorse.

As with all desktop microphones, the Yeti is sensitive to vibrations, so I have mine attached to a Rode microphone stand which clips to my desk to reduce interference.

We are a divided household when it comes to microphones. My husband prefers the Snowball by Blue Mic. Our son prefers the Samson Go Mic. It is an interesting take on the desktop mic as it is designed to clip to the edge of your laptop or monitor. Another contender for favorite microphone is the Raspberry by Blue Mic. This little mic packs a bunch of features into a microphone with a very small footprint.

Figure 3: Raspberry by Blue Mic

In addition to having a port to allow you to hear through headphones, this microphone has multiple modes, including cardioid. It also has an independent gain setting. One of my favorite features of this microphone is the USB cord with a lightning connector. A USB adapter is not required with this microphone.

Desktop microphones can be an investment. Of the mics mentioned, the Raspberry is the most expensive at $199. The Yeti is usually around $130. The Snowball ICE can be found for less than $50. The Samson Go Mic is less than $30.

Although desktop microphones are convenient, not everyone is a fan. Many people prefer headsets or lapel mics.

Headsets and Lapel Mics

Headsets are what most people think of when they envision someone using voice recognition software. The market for this category of microphones is wide open. Gaming consoles have spurred growth in this segment of the market. In fact, some people report that their gaming headsets contain extremely high quality microphones. Gaming microphones are offered at all price points. However, the ONIKUMA K1b Pro Gaming Headset comes with several types of adapters. It's a good deal for less than forty dollars.

An inexpensive noise-canceling microphone is available from Andrea Electronics. The NC-185 is a remarkably good option for around twenty dollars.

It also has split leads which can help reduce background noise.

The Sennheiser SC 630 USB Microphone is a pricier microphone at approximately $120, but it has a mute switch built in and is a unidirectional microphone. Although, I have not used this particular Sennheiser microphone, I have had several other models in the past and can speak to the quality of the components.

The Flexy Mic is considered the cream of the crop when it comes to accurate headsets. Users report that it is comfortable to wear and can be used with digital recorders. With an adapter, you can also use it with your telephone. The Flexy Mic runs approximately $150. However, the recommended adapter to make it USB compatible is also $150. There are cheaper alternatives for 3.5 mm to USB adapters available. I cannot personally speak to the comparative quality of them because the Flexy Mic is still on my wish list.

Before I discovered the Yeti by Blue Mic, I used to use a lot of lapel microphones. I have glasses and it drives me crazy when they interfere with my headset. So, I frequently used lapel microphones. There are a wide variety of them at different price points. It's been a while since I have used them, and I can't recommend a specific brand. However, if possible you want to make sure they are unidirectional and noise canceling. Lapel microphones are particularly susceptible to wind noise and the rustling of your clothes. Make sure you use a foam windscreen on your lapel microphone. Replacement clips can be purchased on sites like Amazon. (There is a good reason I know this. I have a special talent for losing small things.)

Wireless

A surprising number of authors I know like to pace or use a treadmill while dictating. Wireless headphones would be handy in a situation like this. However, there is a cost to using wireless technology. Frequently, you sacrifice clarity. If you absolutely need to use a wireless microphone, Knowbrainer.com recommends the VXi VoxStar UC Bluetooth microphone ($50) or the Sennheiser PRESENCE UC Bluetooth Headset ($150).

Wireless microphones don't always have long battery life when subjected to the rigors of dictation. You can find yourself in the middle of a project when the microphone will suddenly drop your speech. Apparently, the VoxStar is particularly prone to this issue.

 If you plan to use a wireless microphone as your primary input device, I recommend purchasing more than one so you can charge one while using the other.

Interestingly, using the Krisp application, I am able to use my Solo Beats 3 wireless headphones while dictating. The accuracy is not as high as when I use my Yeti by Blue Mic, however it'll do in a pinch.

What in the world is Krisp? If you've never heard of it, let me tell you about what I consider to be the biggest development in all of dictation.

Krisp – A New Choice

If you've spent any time dictating, you know the frustration of ambient background noise interfering with your dictation. I work from home and my people and pets don't always understand when I'm trying to work. This can lead to some interesting dictation results. However, I have stumbled upon the cure for my woes. It is a little application called Krisp. Currently, it is available for Windows and Mac OS. Eventually, they plan to introduce it to iOS and Android. When that happens, the world of transcription will never be the same.

I don't know exactly how Krisp works. However, I do know what it does. It miraculously screens out background noise. No, I really mean it! I am dictating this while music is playing a few inches from my Yeti by Blue Mic. My husband has a habit of watching television in the next room with the volume turned up so loud that it frequently interferes with the quality of my dictation. My dog,

Lily, feels the need to bark at every passing stranger on the street. Now, her barks do not appear in my manuscript as the words will, will, will, will. This app is life changing.

Krisp is a subscription-based program. While I was fortunate enough to score a lifetime deal through AppSumo, I truly believe this software is worth the monthly fee. It is that good.

Practically speaking, Krisp sets up a virtual microphone on your computer. Then, you add to your application (Dragon®, Skype, GoToMeeting, FaceTime, or whatever) as if it is another microphone.

*Figure 4: Adding a Krisp Microphone to Dragon®
Professional Individual 6.0.8*

I have a MacBook Pro and although I mute the internal microphone when I use an external microphone, sometimes it still acts as if it is receiving sound. This application allows you to block the internal microphone as it screens out background noise.

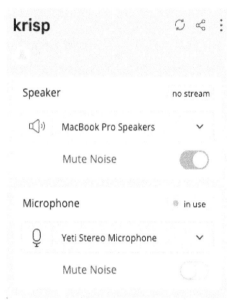

Figure 5: Krisp Virtual Microphone Settings

Did I mention I'm listening to Brett Young with my phone a few inches from my microphone as I dictate this? I've had this program for several days now, I am still astonished by the difference it makes in the quality of my dictation. Life happens around me and I can still work! I can't tell you how valuable that is to me. I firmly believe Krisp represents the biggest advance in dictation technology I've ever seen. The app even turned the mediocre wireless microphone attached to my Solo Beats 3 into a viable dictation source. Although I love my Beats for quality audio, the microphone output is the pits.

I use both the Windows and Mac version of Krisp. They function equally well. The only downside I have discovered is a tiny, almost imperceptible lag. Don't take my word for it. You can participate in an interactive demo and hear for yourself the difference the program makes. Additionally, there is a free trial period.

Now that you've chosen the program and your microphone, we need to choose an appropriate computer.

Chapter 4 – It's Gotta Run on Something - Computer Equipment

One of my pet peeves about Nuance® is while they are talented at selling you software, they are less than forthright when it comes to the minimum specifications of the computer equipment needed to run their programs effectively. This has always been the case. Now, as I mentioned, I'm not a computer scientist or programmer. I'm just an end user. As a consumer of dictation technology, I have seen voice recognition software mature from the barely functional Kurzweil and early versions of Dragon® to the right-out-of-the-box accuracy Nuance® can now rightfully brag about.

Quite frankly, Nuance®'s minimum equipment requirements are a joke. Regardless of which version of Dragon® you run, it is a memory intensive program which is designed to run with other resource hogs.

I am sharing my frustration in hopes that you won't be suckered into purchasing less than adequate hardware for the demands Dragon® will put on it. Nuance® claims that Dragon® can be run on a machine with 4 GB of RAM. This may work if Dragon® was the only program running on your whole computer. However, we all know operating systems and word processors take memory and processing power.

So, let's be practical and realistic, shall we?

Under no circumstances do I recommend running either version of Dragon® Professional Individual on anything with less than 8 GB of RAM. Even that configuration is a stretch and may lead to unacceptable lag. 16 GB of RAM and an i7 processor with a solid-state drive are more in line with what you will actually need to be happy with Dragon® Professional Individual.

The capabilities of your machine make a marked difference. Recently, I was able to upgrade my MacBook Pro when Apple was unable to fix a manufacturing problem on my laptop. I now have a MacBook Pro with 32 GB of RAM and an i9 processor. I expected it to be fast, but I've also noticed the extra processing power means my computer doesn't lock up as much and I spend much less time staring at spinning beach balls. Now, Dragon® just runs like it's supposed to and crashes less often.

I can hear you yelling at the computer screen from here. "Mary, 32 GB of RAM is ridiculous and so far out of my budget I can't even see it!"

Trust me, I get it. Even though more powerful models are preferred, Dragon® Professional Individual will run on less powerful machines. I have it running on my 8 GB MacBook Pro. It's slow, but it works. So, if you can't upgrade your computer at this point, never fear. However, when you are in the market for a new computer, keep in mind that Dragon® is a memory intensive program.

So, let's look at individual systems and determine exactly what you need to put on your wish list.

PCs and Other Windows Devices

To a certain extent, which PC you get is a matter of personal taste. I am exceptionally hard on computers. I'm not exactly sure why, but regardless of the brand, I seem to have issues. Consequently, I usually purchase Dell computers with the most comprehensive warranty. Many times, a Dell technician will come to my house to fix what I've screwed up. I like this service. So, I continue to purchase Dell computers.

Here are the features you need to look for when you purchase a PC.

A minimum of 8 GB, but preferably 16 GB of RAM.

- An i7 or better processor.
- A solid-state hard drive.
- If you are using a laptop, it is helpful to have a quiet fan.

These days, it is not common to find CD drives built into laptop computers. If you need one to load your programs, you can purchase them inexpensively on Amazon.

There are other considerations worth noting. If you're anything like me, you spend a lot of time staring at your computer screen. So, if you're choosing a laptop, all other things being equal, look for a screen with high pixel density.

If you can, look for a PC which will allow you to increase the amount of RAM. Someday, you might appreciate the flexibility.

For those looking for a specific recommendation, my Dell XPS has been a workhorse. It has a nifty convertible screen which is great for making presentations.

Several authors I know report great success using the Microsoft Surface 6. The cost of the newest version ranges from $699 to $2,000. The high-end machines are quite powerful with 16 GB of RAM and a terabyte of hard drive space. Avid owners of the Microsoft Surface tout its extreme portability as their favorite feature.

Mac

Up until four years ago, I was a diehard Windows user. Then, I discovered Mac. As I have established, I dictate a bunch. So, I have been through several Mac computers. They all still function. My son is using my 2013 hand-me-down computer in high school.

Initially, I started out with a Mac mini. It is Apple's version of a desktop computer. Currently, you can get a model with 16 GB of RAM, a 1 TB solid-state drive and an i7 processor for around $1,800. You will have to buy a monitor, keyboard and touchpad or mouse separately.

I recommend Samsung curved monitors because they really reduce eye fatigue. These run about two hundred dollars.

I didn't plan far enough ahead when I purchased my Mac Mini, and I quickly ran out of hard drive space.

 Always get more processing power and hard drive space than you think you'll need.

As far as laptops go, there are two options in Apple's lineup.

The MacBook Air is light and compact. It has a beautiful display and can be customized to include up to 16 GB of RAM and a 512 GB hard drive. The processor is equivalent to an i7. This configuration will run you approximately $1,800 new.

I recently upgraded my MacBook Pro to a 32 GB i9 processor with a terabyte hard drive. I am thrilled with its processing speed. I have absolutely no lag whatsoever. Do you need to upgrade to 32 GB? Maybe not. But, it is *so* cool! Dragon® freezes up less when I use my 32 GB machine versus my old one with 16 GB of RAM.

A 13-inch MacBook Pro with 16 GB of RAM and an i9 processor with a 512 GB hard drive will cost you approximately $2,000. For about three hundred dollars more, you can get a 15.4-inch model. The Retina display on these computers is phenomenal.

As I said, my son is currently using my 2013 MacBook Pro. It still runs like a champ. If there's anyone harder on computers than I am, it is my youngest son.

 Regardless of which model of Mac computer you choose, I strongly recommend that you purchase an AppleCare policy.

So, the question must be asked: if Dragon® Professional Individual 6.0.8 has been discontinued, why bother to get a Mac?

I use three applications which make the Mac worth a few extra hundred: Scrivener 3, Photoshop, and Vellum. Although the first two programs have Windows counterparts, Vellum does not. If you do not have a Mac computer, you need to pay a fee for a service like Mac in Cloud to use Vellum.

Perhaps a Little of Both – Virtual Desktops

It is now possible to get the best of both worlds. As we speak, I am operating Windows on my MacBook Pro. What's more, I can seamlessly move between platforms. I am perfectly happy using the Mac OS most of the time. However, sometimes people will have questions about Dragon® Professional Individual 15.3 or Scrivener for Windows. In order to answer them with authority, I often need to problem solve in Windows. Prior to adopting desktop virtualization software, this would require someone to fetch my Windows computer and locate the charger for me. It was just a huge hassle. Now, I just click on a button and I am in Windows land.

In this picture, I have Scrivener 3 for Mac up on one side of the screen while I am dictating into Speech Productivity Pro using Dragon® Professional Individual 15.3 for Windows.

I resisted this technology for a long time because I am not very confident in my skills as a computer nerd. I was afraid desktop virtualization software would be cumbersome and difficult to use. I can't speak to every desktop virtualization program out there, as I've only used Parallels Desktop® 15 for Mac Home Edition. I found it incredibly easy to set up and use.

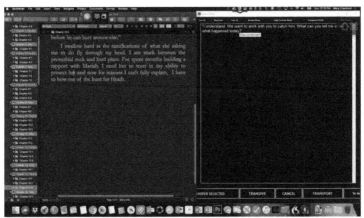

Figure 6: Scrivener 3 for Mac together with Speech Productivity Pro and Dragon® Professional Individual 15.3

I purchased a license for Windows because I wanted to be able to customize the look and settings of Windows 10. However, if that is not important to you, you don't even need to purchase an additional license for Windows.

Parallels has a variety of price points and offers a discount for educators. The Home Edition requires a one-time fee, while the Pro edition is a yearly subscription.

There are other desktop virtualization software programs available – and some of them are free.

These include VMware Workstation and Oracle VM VirtualBox.

These virtual desktops are resource intensive. If your computer does not have a lot of RAM or processing power, this may not be a solution for you.

Speech to Text Applications for Your Phone or Tablet

A lot of writers would love to be productive while away from the computer. Dictation makes that possible. Stuck in a school pickup line? No problem! Have a little time on your lunch hour but want to get out of the office for a change? Got you covered. Want to go for a walk with the dog and visit the park? That's doable too.

There are two ways to go about this. You can use your phone, tablet or iPad together with a dictation application.

In my opinion, a more productive option is to use the transcription feature within your desktop version of Dragon® Professional Individual. Both the Windows and Mac version have streamlined the transcription process and made great improvements over earlier versions.

If you want to dictate directly into an application and see your words appear on the screen, programs like GoogleDocs, SpeechNotes, Speechy, and Dragon® Anywhere are all at your disposal. However, not all speech to text applications are created equal.

As discussed before, Google Docs has some real limitations under the desktop version. However, many of those are not present in the IOS version. One thing that remains, however, is the time limit on dictation. After just a couple of paragraphs, I find that the program quits on me – sometimes, in the middle of a thought. This is not ideal. However, Google Docs is free.

SpeechNotes has both a web-based app attached to Google Chrome, and an Android app. SpeechNotes has relatively good accuracy. That's a good thing, because you cannot correct your mistakes by voice. Additionally, SpeechNotes is subject to the same limitations on blue language as Google Docs. SpeechNotes has both a free version and a premium version available for a one-time fee of $9.99. Unlike many other applications, with the premium version, you can dictate in dark mode.

Among the most impressive applications I have tried to date is called Speechy. As nearly as I can tell, it is only available for iOS. It has some features which make it stand out from the crowd. First, you can dictate punctuation and cuss words with abandon. Secondly, it is easy to export your files to another app or to your computer. Lastly, it records your dictation at the same time it records your speech files. You can export both.

These phone apps are fun and helpful, however most of them are not designed for power users. Although I have issues with the quality of Dragon® Anywhere compared to the full desktop versions of Dragon® Professional Individual, it is still by far and away the most powerful speech to text tool available for iOS, android and tablets. It really is second to none.

Dragon® Anywhere

 Dragon Anywhere is still the most powerful speech to text tool out there. The app is available for iOS and Android phones and tablets. It really is second to none.

As I discussed above, Dragon® Anywhere is the speech to text application to beat. Nothing else comes close. However, for a price tag of $15 a month or $150 per year, it is understandable that Dragon® Anywhere outperforms all of its competition.

Dragon® Anywhere is the only speech to text program which will allow you to edit your document with your voice and make corrections. Additionally, it learns from corrections and you can make a custom vocabulary. Further, it syncs that vocabulary across all of your Dragon® applications. If you work in multiple places, this is a godsend. It ensures your custom vocabulary is always up-to-date.

The correction mechanism is a little clunky and not as accessible as I would like it to be. However, that does not negate the fact that Dragon® Anywhere is the most powerful speech to text mobile app available. It works on both iOS and Android.

SpeechNotes

SpeechNotes, a web-based application, is an extension to Chrome. It also is available as an app for Android. Although some punctuation is available, it is somewhat limited. Additionally, you will be subject to the censorship present in Google Docs. The program itself is quite accurate, which is a good thing since you cannot make corrections with your voice.

SpeechNotes has also introduced a beta transcription service. You buy credits which are then used depending upon the length of your dictation.

Although you can dictate punctuation such as quotation marks, commas, semicolons and colons, in the desktop version, you cannot do this in the Android version. Additionally, if you need a capital letter in a word which is otherwise not capitalized, you are sorry out of luck. Additionally, you cannot use commands like indent.

Speechy

There is a lot to like about the Speechy IOS app. It has many unusual bells and whistles. The accuracy is relatively high. You can dictate full punctuation with this app and cuss with abandon. It saves both your dictation work and your speech files. This is a helpful feature if you ever need to compare the written file with your audio. The app has a real-time translation tool which sets it apart from the rest of the contenders. There is a time limit on the free version, however it is removed once you upgrade to Pro for $6.99.

One of my favorite features of this program is its ability to export both dictation and speech files. You can drop them into Dropbox, send them to yourself in an email, or if you have a Mac, you can choose to use AirDrop. Unfortunately, like many of these speech-to-text applications, there doesn't seem to be a way to correct your mistakes using your voice. You have to use your keyboard.

Voice Notebook

Voice Notebook is available for both Android and iOS. It is based on Google's speech engine. So, it is subject to the same sort of limitations. Punctuation is limited and you cannot make corrections by voice. The price for the Pro version is $3.99. It's files are exported in .txt form. The app's accuracy is adequate, but there are better options for speech to text options out there.

Otter.ai

There has been a lot of buzz in the dictation community about Otter.ai. Although it's intended to transcribe meetings and conference calls, some authors are using it to record dictation. There is a free version of the app which allows for six hundred minutes of transcription for free. Otherwise, a six-thousand-minute plan is available for ten dollars a month.

Initially, I was intrigued – until I actually used it. It is very disconcerting. Because I lack breath support, I frequently pause during my dictation. This does not work well in Otter.ai. It causes the program to treat each phrase as a different speaker. Additionally, the program doesn't recognize punctuation such as quotation marks, semicolons and colons.

Although this is a unique application with great potential for other uses, it is not very practical for long passages of dictation.

Figure 7: Dictating into Otter.ai

Transcription Tools

Many authors find transcription is quicker than dictating into a speech to text application because they are not focused on correcting mistakes. The ability to hold a device and just talk without focusing on the form of the product is incredibly freeing.

Most of the time when I discuss features in Dragon®, if you use an older version on the same platform, it doesn't matter much. Transcription is the exception. When I speak about transcription, I am talking about the latest versions of Dragon® Professional Individual. In recent years, they have made dramatic changes to the transcription functions. If you plan to use your Dragon® program primarily as a tool to help with transcription, it is a good idea to upgrade to the latest version for your platform. The transcription tools are much more powerful now than they used to be.

Digital Recorders

These days, there are lots of digital recorders out there. Ideally, you should choose one with clear, easy-to-understand buttons, the ability to expand memory, and an easy mechanism to store and name files.

The Sony ICDUX560BLK Digital Voice Recorder gets high marks for its clear, easy to use controls and quick charge capability.

The SAIMPU Voice Recorder-16GB Voice Activated Recorder with Variable Speed Playback is a popular model because of its toughness and clear recording sound. It is a mono recorder which is best for transcription.

Finally, the Olympus Voice Recorder WS-853 commonly ranks at the top of the list for digital voice recorders. The only time I have had difficulty with mine is when I inadvertently plugged the external microphone into the wrong port.

 Regardless of which brand of recorder you choose, make sure you charge it before you go on a long transcription quest. There's nothing like distorted files to dampen your enthusiasm.

Also, you may want to practice with your new recording device to make sure you know what each button does and when to use it. I know, it seems pretty straightforward. However, when you are in the emotion of the moment and concentrating on writing, sometimes complicated technology ruins your flow. So, I would recommend practicing with your digital recorder. You should know in advance what each button does and how to create an audio file. This will make it much easier to operate when you get lost in your story. If you're anything like me, you don't ever use a digital recorder unless your occupation requires it.

Phone Applications

Although I own two digital recorders, my favorite way to record files for transcription is with my phone. I don't transcribe much, but when I do it's usually when I haven't planned ahead. Like most people, the one constant technology in my life is my smart phone. Unlike my digital recorders, I carry my phone with me and it's usually charged. Using a phone app to transcribe takes away my excuse not to sneak in a few words when I have unexpected down time.

There are several applications available to record your speech. Look for one that allows you to control the type of audio file available for export. Additionally, it is helpful if you can set the gain and choose names for your files and categorize them somehow.

By far and away, my favorite recording application for the phone or tablet is Voice Record Pro.

Voice Record Pro

I don't always have a recorder with me when I need it the most. However, I almost always carry my iPhone.

Voice Record Pro is a simple, straightforward application which allows a great deal of flexibility. It is available for both iOS and Android. This program allows you to automatically send your files to Dropbox, One Drive, Google Drive and many others. You can choose to email it to yourself. I find I am more likely transcribe my files when I don't have to worry about how to get them transferred to the computer.

Voice Record Pro allows you to choose the format in which your audio files are saved. This is a very handy feature.

Other applications I have used require you to convert your audio files into a usable form for transcription. The acceptable formats for transcription with Dragon® include .wav, .mp3, .wma, .dss, .ds2, and .m4a. Voice Record Pro also has settings to boost your gain and set your silence tolerance. It is a supremely customizable program for recording.

The Windows version of Dragon® Professional Individual allows you to batch process transcription in the background. The only caveat is you must not be using the program for dictation at the same time. There are two ways to transcribe in Dragon Professional Individual 15.3. Regardless of what method you use to transcribe, always move your audio files from your recording device to your computer first. Don't try to transcribe directly from your digital recorder.

If you want to process one file at a time, you can go to the menu bar and choose Tools and then click Transcribe Recording. If you would like to transcribe several files, you can elect to use the Auto Transcribe Folder Agent. To access this tool, choose 'Tools' and then click on 'Auto Transcribe Folder Agent'. Once you click on the tool, create a new task. Set the input directory and an output directory. It is helpful to clearly identify these folders as raw audio data and converted files. I just specific files using Windows Explorer. Next, choose the type of file you would like. Dragon to output. You can choose from .txt, .rtf, or .doc, Click 'OK'.

The last step is to use the DragonBar to exit Dragon. Simply click on the DragonBar and then 'Exit Dragon'. You must exit Dragon® because your profile cannot be doing two things at once. The Auto Transcribe Folder Agent will run in the background. But, you won't be able to use your profile in Dragon® to dictate. After you have the Auto Transcribe Folder Agent set up, drag or copy your audio files into the input folder you specified. Now, the tool can transcribe your files in the background while you do other things with your computer. Your microphone will have a big gray X to remind you that it is not available while you are Transcribing.

If you correct any mistakes Dragon® makes in recognizing your speech, over time your profiles will become more accurate. At one point, it was believed that you couldn't train your files on the Mac version if you were doing transcription. This is not true. If Dragon® mis-recognizes what you said, it is important to take the time to correct the misunderstanding.

Keep in mind, editing for Dragon®'s misrecognitions is not the same as editing for clarity. Those are different processes.

Traditional Transcription

Several authors I know don't bother to use the transcription function within Dragon® Professional Individual at all. They record their audio files and hand them off to someone else to do the transcribing. Several companies on the Internet offer machine based transcription services for a fee. This is usually based on the length of your audio files. Still others hand their recordings off to a real life transcriptionist. There is a real benefit to using an actual human being in the process. Our brains can decipher the difference between words far better than artificial intelligence. Additionally, humans can filter out background noise in a way that transcription software cannot. The downside is that transcription can be a spendy option. However, many who use it swear it saves them enough time that their increased productivity offsets the cost.

Personally, I have never used these transcription services. I caution you to choose carefully if you are using a company online. Make sure to study their privacy policies and recourse if something goes wrong.

Chapter 5 – Protect Your Work - Speech Productivity Pro

Dragon®Pad is included in both the Windows and Mac version of Dragon® Professional Individual. It has been a key component of Dragon® since almost the beginning. It is a clipboard within Dragon® and it allows you to dictate into programs which are not otherwise supported by Dragon®. Quite frankly, this inclues almost all programs (with the exception of a handful of products). Dragon® has full text control for most Microsoft Office products, Open Office, LibreOffice, WordPerfect, and Scrivener 3 for Mac. If you need to dictate in another program, Dragon® will open Dragon®Pad so you can dictate directly into it and copy and paste into your application. I have one simple word:

Don't!

Okay, you may think I'm being overly dramatic. But I swear to you I am not. Over thirty years, I have lost thousands and thousands of words because:

Dragon®Pad is prone to crashing. Unlike when Dragon® Professional Individual 6.0.8 crashes, if Dragon®Pad crashes, it takes everything with it.

So, what is a cautious author to do?

This is one of those cases where the version of Dragon® Professional Individual you are using matters. On the Mac side, I dictate into Grammarly when I am not dictating in a program which supports full text support. Other options include Notes or Text Edit (which come standard with your operating system). The advantage to using Grammarly or Notes is that they are automatically backed up as you are using the program. So, if something catastrophic happens to Dragon® or your system in general, you won't lose as much data. Grammarly requires Internet access for it to work properly.

If you are using Dragon® Professional Individual 15.3, I recommend Speech Productivity Pro.

Speech Productivity Pro is everything Dragon®Pad should be, but isn't. In my opinion, it is the single best way to protect yourself from data loss when you are using Dragon® Professional Individual 15.3. It is an add-on program, but the peace of mind is invaluable. The standard version will cost you $25 and the Pro version is $45. I like the Pro version because the windows are extremely sharp and customizable. Speech Productivity will work with the professional versions of Dragon® 10 or higher. It won't work with the basic, home or premium editions or on a Mac.

In addition to being able to choose the font size and size of your box, Speech Productivity Pro allows you to choose the background. My favorite mode is called No Headache. However, you can also have a standard white background, a transparent background or one designed for people with visual impairments. The transparent background is really helpful if you're working on an already existing document and want to see what you've already written.

Before you dictate, you should choose a name for your file in Notepad. The file is continuously backed up, helping to ensure no data will be lost even if Dragon® crashes. You can also use this program like a large clipboard and transfer text directly into whatever program you are using. One of the most exciting features of this program is the advanced dictation box. It allows you to format the text as you wish. You can include italics or bold print or even add a bulleted list or pictures. The advanced dictation box allows you to do most of your formatting before you even transfer your data to another application.

In short, Speech Productivity Pro makes it a lot easier and safer to use Dragon® Professional Individual 15.3.

Now that you know which program to use, the equipment to use it on, and ways to keep your work safe, I will discuss programs which are helpful to authors and indicate how Dragon® Professional Individual interacts with them.

Chapter 6 – Where to Put Your Words - Helpful Tools

There are many programs which are helpful to authors. I am going to discuss a few of them and how they interact with Dragon® Professional Individual. This is not meant to be an exhaustive list. I've Included some of the more popular tools for authors.

ProWritingAid

ProWritingAid is my favorite grammar checker. So, you might wonder why I am talking about grammar checkers in conjunction with voice recognition software. There are a few distinct advantages to dictating directly into grammar checking software like ProWritingAid. You can catch mistakes as you make them.

Figure 8: Using Dragon® with ProWritingAid

Grammar checks are especially important when you use Dragon®. Sometimes Dragon® does not always correctly recognize the proper tense. For example, it frequently misses the word I've and writes I instead.

Dictating in an application like ProWritingAid is quicker than working with Microsoft Word.

I am using version 2.0.31 of the Desktop version for Mac together with Dragon® Professional Individual 6.0.8. Most of the time, I have no issues whatsoever. However, if you have done some heavy corrections, Dragon® can lose its place and leave random numbers and letters around. To correct this, simply say, *Cache Document.*

Dragon® Professional Individual works just fine in the web-based version of ProWritingAid as well.

ProWritingAid can be purchased for $70 per year or $240 for lifetime access. Keep an eye out for specials. A couple of years ago, I purchased a lifetime license for significantly less through Appsumo.

As much as I like ProWritingAid for editing my books, it is not my favorite application for direct dictation. For most things, I dictate directly into Grammarly.

Grammarly

I use Grammarly for all sorts of things. The least of which is checking grammar. I love the interface. It makes it really easy to use the program for quick, accessible notes as well as longer documents. There is even a search feature to allow you to find a past document.

New	Freedom - new blurb 7/19	Hearts Set Free new blurb 7/19	The Long Road to Love new blurb 7/19	Pieces new blurb 7/19	Rectify new blurb 7/19
Upload		4			1
Love Claimed - new blurb 7/19	Love Seasoned - new blurb 7/19	Love Naturally - new blurb 7/19	Joy and Tiers - new blurb 7/19	Until the Stars Fall from the Sky - new blurb 7/19	So the Heart Can Dance - new blurb 7/19
	2	1	5		3
If You Know Me - new blurb 7/19	The Price of Freedom - new blurb 7/19	Dreams Change - new blurb 7/19	The Letter - new blurb 7/19	Tempting Fate - new blurb 7/19	Heart Wish - new blurb 7/19
4					
Paths Not Taken - new blurb 7/19	Jude's Song new blurb 7/19	Tough new blurb 7/19	Sheltered Hearts new blurb 7/19	The Power of Will - new blurb 7/19	Port in the Storm new blurb 7/19

Figure 9: Document Organization with Grammarly

When it comes to checking grammar, I prefer ProWritingAid. But for ease of use with Dragon® Professional Individual, Grammarly wins hands down.

Before I started using Scrivener 3 and Speech Productivity Pro, Grammarly was my go to dictation platform. It's faster than using Microsoft Word and everything is automatically backed up. So, if you have a computer malfunction, your work is still there. You do need Wi-Fi access to use Grammarly. If I don't have Wi-Fi access, I use my phone's hotspot. I have full-text control when I use Grammarly. So, if I make a mistake, it is easy enough to fix. I haven't noticed Dragon® Professional Individual 6.0.8 losing its place after I make corrections. You can also turn off the assistant's feedback until you are ready for it. The dictation environment is pleasant and clutter-free.

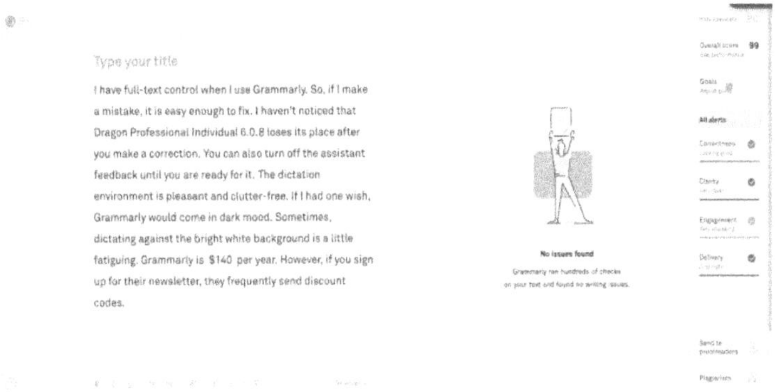

Figure 10: Using Grammarly with
Dragon® Professional Individual

If I had one wish, Grammarly would come in dark mode. Sometimes, dictating against the bright white background is a little fatiguing. Grammarly is $140 per year. However, if you sign up for their newsletter, they frequently send discount codes.

Scrivener

With Scrivener, you can keep track of your manuscript, audio tracks, websites, pictures, and source documents all in one place.

Have you ever run across a piece of software which completely changes the way you approach things? That was my experience with Scrivener. Initially, I started out on the Windows version of Scrivener. At the time, Scrivener 3 for Mac was a much more comprehensive program. So, I switched platforms to be able to use it. Literature and Latte is working on making the Windows version of Scrivener just as powerful. They are expected to release a new version for Windows soon.

I love being able to see the organization of my work with a single glance. With Scrivener, you can keep track of your manuscript, audio tracks, websites, pictures, and source documents all in one place. I can also manipulate the appearance and output of my projects without affecting the manuscript. I format all my own books using Scrivener. The most important thing is that using Scrivener is far quicker than dictating in Microsoft Word. There is virtually no lag time.

Some people are hesitant to use Scrivener because they have heard that it has a steep learning curve. I'm not sure Scrivener is difficult, it's more that people are used to working with programs like Microsoft Word because that's the way they were taught in school.

I like to envision Scrivener like one big Trapper Keeper. For those of you not of my generation, a Trapper Keeper was a huge binder with several sections. You could add things like calendars, rulers, pencil holders and even a calculator that fit into the binder. When you were done, you just zipped it all together and everything was organized. Scrivener is a lot like that. There are many parts to Scrivener, but you don't have to understand it all to begin using it.

The first section is the binder. This is what it sounds like. It is where you keep your manuscript, research materials and background information like character sheets.

I have a model book I've created which is set up the way I like to work. Whenever I start a new project, I simply use save as and use the new novel name. Then, I use project replace to change out the character names. That way, I don't have to keep reinventing the wheel every time I start a new novel.

Figure 11: Binder Structure for Novel in Scrivener 3

 If you already have a document you started somewhere else and want to use it in Scrivener, that's not an issue. You can use the import and split function to have your document automatically divided into folders.

It is important to understand that the scrivenings (the part that looks like a traditional word processor), the cork board, and the outline are simply three ways to look at the same material. So, if you make a change to your index card on the cork board, the change will be reflected in your binder, outline and scrivenings.

Figure 12: Scrivenings View

Figure 13: Corkboard View

Figure 14: Outline View

The research tab in your binder serves as a catchall. You can drag websites into it and have instant access. Are your characters inspired by a particular kind of music? You can place music files in your research tab. Building character or location sheets is easy in Scrivener using their templates. The research folder is where I place my cover.

The third major function of Scrivener is compile.

The compile feature allows you to output your file in a dozen different ways. You can create EPUB, MOBI, PDF or Word or Open Office files.

You can also compile just part of your document. Let's say you are entering a contest and need the first four chapters. That's not a challenge for Scrivener. You can do that without having to copy and paste a single thing.

This is not meant to be a tutorial on Scrivener, I just wanted to illustrate my point to help you understand a little bit about how Scrivener 3 works.

The effectiveness of Dragon® Professional Individual in Scrivener depends upon which platform you are using.

 If you are using a Mac, Dragon® Professional Individual 6.0.8 works perfectly with Scrivener 3. You can dictate directly into Scrivener 3 regardless of which view you prefer. You don't need to copy and paste in the Mac version.

This is my favorite feature. I have full text control in Scrivener 3. I can correct my mistakes and edit the document.

Working with Scrivener for Windows and Dragon® Professional Individual 15.3 is a different story. Although you can technically dictate into Scrivener for Windows, it lacks full text control which makes correcting and editing a document difficult.

When I use the Windows version of Scrivener, I use another application and then copy and paste my results into Scrivener. Speech Productivity Pro is my favorite application for this purpose.

However, Grammarly, OneNote, Notepad, or text edit work fine as well. Sadly, Dragon®'s performance is not any better in the beta version of Scrivener 3 for Windows. It is my hope that Nuance® will figure out that a lot of people write using Scrivener and introduce full-text control to the Windows version.

Many people who use Scrivener are also fans of Scrapple, a mind mapping program, and Aeon, a timeline program.

If you use a Mac, you will be able to dictate directly into both programs. However, if you are using Dragon® Professional Individual 15.3, you will need to use another application to copy and paste your information into either program. Neither of them offer full text control.

Vellum

Vellum is a Mac-based program. It is not available for Windows. It is most known for its formatting abilities. However, many authors I know write their novels directly in Vellum and don't bother to use another program like Scrivener or Microsoft Word.

The advantage of this approach is that you can see in real time what your finished product will look like. This feature might work well if you are typing, however Vellum is a terrible platform to use with Dragon® Professional Individual 6.0.8. Unfortunately, Dragon® loses its place and has no text control. Even though you can technically dictate directly into Vellum, doing so will mean you have no ability to correct mistakes.

In short, Vellum a great tool for formatting your books, but it doesn't play well with Dragon®.

Novlr

Novlr is a web-based tool designed to help authors write books. The interface is stunningly simple. It has a focus mode in which you can eliminate all distractions. It has a dark mode, which I truly appreciate. In the evening mode, the text is bright yellow. One thoughtful feature is the ability to set it to automatically use curly quotes. This app is very intuitive. It's beauty is in its simplicity.

You can add a chapter at a time and there is a separate section for notes. You could label these notes anything you want to.

 Everything is automatically backed up in Novlr – even across platforms. This feature works even off-line.

For example, when I went to test the program on the Windows side of things, when I went back to using my Mac, the program asked me if I wanted to save the new version instead of the old one. This feature is handy if you are dictating in more than one environment.

I have no problems using Novlr with Dragon® Professional Individual 6.0.8. It allows me to have full text control and make corrections.

When I switched over to Windows, initially I had difficulty dictating with Dragon® Professional Individual 15.3 while using Microsoft Edge. However, when I installed Google Chrome, dictation worked just fine and I had full text control and the ability to make corrections.

Novlr is a subscription-based service and costs $10 per month or $100 per year.

The bottom line is that it is a simple, straightforward writing app which works well with both the Mac and Windows version of Dragon®. It offers convenient syncing and saving abilities and an aesthetically pleasing interface.

Dabble

Dabble is a web-based service intended to help you structure your novel and write without a lot of interference on the screen. There's lots to like about it. Because it is web-based, your work is automatically saved. You can move from computer to computer without disrupting your work. Dabble is a distraction-free interface and it offers a basic format for a novel. You can add chapters and scenes as well as character sheets and plot points. You can choose to use it in dark mode. It exports your documents into Microsoft Word. Now, for the not so great parts; Dabble charges $9.99 or $99 a year to use their service. There is no android or iOS version.

I had no issues using Dabble with Dragon® Professional Individual 6.0.8. However, when I went over to the Windows side, full punctuation was available, but correction abilities were limited.

I like the structure of this app, however the same could be replicated in a less expensive, non-subscription-based service like Scrivener.

StoryShop

StoryShop is another web-based storytelling app. It is much more complicated to use than Novlr or Dabble. It seems to take the opposite approach and pack its program with tons of options. For example in the pro version, there are beat templates, character templates, location templates, world building tools and it's built for collaborating.

The character sheets are incredibly detailed and allow you to upload photographs. They also allow you to establish interrelationships between characters. For example, you can identify partners, parents, siblings. If you are like me and carry your characters forward from novel to novel, this is a very helpful feature.

I had no difficulty using either version of Dragon® Professional Individual with StoryShop. I had full text control and could correct my mistakes with ease.

If you would like to try StoryShop, they have a lite version available for free. The Pro version is $9.99 per month or $99 per year.

Ulysses

Ulysses is a popular application among some authors. It is available for Mac and iOS. It has some helpful features like dark mode and a typewriter scrolling feature, which is nice to keep your text in the middle of the screen as you dictate.

You can use markup to give your sections headings and other formatting.

As cool as this application is, it is one of the least responsive with Dragon® Professional Individual 6.0.8. I don't have the ability to correct mistakes or even select text. I can technically dictate into this application, but it is not practically functional with Dragon®. There are more dictation friendly applications out there. If you want to check it out yourself, Ulysses offers a free three day trial.

Microsoft Word

At this point, many of you are probably asking, "What's wrong with using Microsoft Word? It's a word processor, after all."

It is a word processor. Even better, most of us are familiar with how it works. You can use headings to build an outline, index and table of contents. It is remarkably flexible and easy to customize. So ... what's not to like?

Despite being one of the programs Nuance® specifically identifies as having full text control, Microsoft Word does not always work particularly well with Dragon®. If your document is short with not a lot of tables and graphics, Dragon® tends to cope better. However, as your file size grows, so does the lag as you are dictating. Additionally, there are web-based versions of Office 365 which are incompatible with Dragon® Professional Individual.

 If you are using Dragon® Professional Individual 6.0.8, editing Microsoft Word for Mac can be a challenge since Dragon® doesn't work with the commenting function.

Initially, when I was testing to see which features were operational in Office 365 on the Windows side, I wasn't able to dictate using Dragon® Professional Individual 15.3 at all. So, I uninstalled Office completely and reinstalled it. After I did that, I was able to dictate in Microsoft Word for Windows. It had a pretty significant lag time. However, I was able to exercise full control and correct my mistakes. It seems that when I installed Office 365, it installed the web based version. Additionally, the commenting feature works with Dragon® Professional Individual 15.3.

So, if Microsoft Word is your jam, there are some things you can do to ensure Dragon® works better. First, make sure you've closed any applications you are not using. This includes your web browser. Break your file up into small sections. Dragon® stores dictation in its cache to make it easier to make corrections. So, if you keep your document size small, it helps a great deal. Additionally, if you have to insert tables and graphics, you might want to do that at the end after you have finished dictating.

Prices for Office 365 vary greatly. Microsoft offers many discount programs for educational use and for members of the military.

OneNote

 OneNote is an incredibly flexible tool. You can use it to take notes, save information from the web, outline and create a story bible.

I would be remiss if I didn't mention the usefulness of OneNote. The ways to organize it are practically endless and it is web-based so you can have access anywhere. Dragon® Professional Individual operates in full text control in OneNote. You can make corrections and have a full complement of formatting options while using this application.

Pages

Pages is the built-in word processor on the Mac operating system. I don't know why I don't use it more often. Dragon® Professional Individual 6.0.8 works extremely well with Pages. It does not have the lag that is present with Microsoft Word.

It has an impressive array of predefined templates which are easy to customize to your needs. For example, this is their traditional novel template.

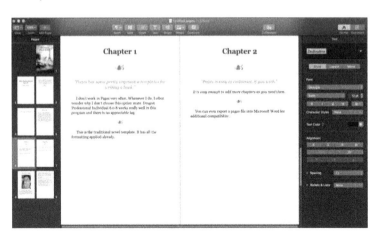

Figure 15: Dictating into Pages

This program allows you to export your Pages file into many different formats. Additionally, you can publish directly to Apple Books right from the Pages application.

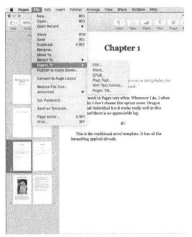

Figure 16: Exporting Options in Pages

If you want an easy to use application to use with your Mac, Pages might be just what you're looking for.

Chapter 7 – Other Helpful Applications

Tomato One

The most benign of these time management tools is Tomato One. It is a Pomodoro timer for your computer. I can set it to dictate for fifty minutes and take a ten minute break. Honestly, some days my endurance isn't that great and I need to set the timer for fifteen minutes with a ten minute break. The great thing about Tomato One is that it allows you the flexibility to change both the time and/or the break period. It puts a countdown clock in your menu bar. You can set it to interrupt you when the timer is finished. Additionally, it keeps statistics on how many Pomodoro sessions you have done each day. It is a gentle reminder to put your butt in your chair and your face in front of a microphone.

Tomato One is a free app for the Mac platform. A similar program for Windows is called Tomato - Be Focused. It is also free.

Focus and Focus Me

 I find Focus to be an absolutely invaluable tool when I am chasing a deadline.

It's quite possible that a simple timer won't be enough to overcome your tendencies to surf the web. In that case, I recommend Focus (Mac) or Focus Me (Mac, Windows, and Android). These programs can be used as stopwatches for sprinting, but they also actively block websites.

In addition to the sites you would expect like Facebook, Pinterest, Instagram and Tumblr. They can also be set to block Amazon, Esty and eBay. Additionally, you can add the sites which distract you from writing. You can choose the amount of time you want websites to be blocked. Additionally, you can set the number of breaks you want within a 24-hour period.

These sites also have different levels of severity. If you really struggle to stay off the Internet, you can choose to go into more of a lockdown mode. At its most severe level, you are not allowed to stop the timer or ease the lock out rules. I don't usually operate under those rules because sometimes you need to be able to access the web for research or to deal with a problem. However, it is an available setting if you need that kind of structure.

I find Focus to be an absolutely invaluable tool when I am chasing a deadline. Focus has several tiers of programming and can be purchased for as little as $19 or as much as $149. Focus Me is $2.50 per month or $119.99 for lifetime access.

Now that you have a complete overview of the external tools, we need to focus on the biggest tool of all: your mindset.

Chapter 8 – It's All in How You Think

Successfully using dictation as a tool is more than just about the external equipment you use – even though those choices are important. It involves changing your mindset and challenging yourself to try new things. I'll discuss a few mental barriers to dictation. Some of these may resonate with you, while others may make no sense. Not everyone has the same stumbling blocks.

Dictation is Just Another Input Mechanism

 Dictation is just another input method. That may seem like a simple concept, but some people get hung up on how they write instead of what they write.

Dictation is simply another input tool. That may seem obvious, but some people can get hung up on how they write instead of what they write. So, I'm going to address some of the common misconceptions and fears that often accompanies the use of voice recognition software.

Relax, You're Still a Writer

I have been dictating almost as long as the technology has existed. I have to be honest with you, I don't understand the controversy around dictation in the writing community. When I first heard someone say that dictating wasn't "real" writing, I was stunned. In fact, I thought I must have misheard the person. Then, I read the same criticism on a couple of writing boards. There it was again, in black-and-white. Someone really said out loud that if you dictate it's not actually the same as writing. I guess somehow it's not hard-core enough. By that logic, we should all be writing with quills and iron salt ink. Tools improve and get better over time. I'm here to tell you more than thirty books later, I work just as hard as an author who dictates as someone who writes longhand or uses a computer keyboard. Dictation is just a different input mechanism – it does not make your process inferior.

Retraining Your Brain to Think Out Loud

 Don't worry if dictation doesn't feel comfortable at first. It takes a while for your brain to get used to thinking creatively while speaking.

Verbalizing creative thoughts is different from writing for business. It requires practice. That is okay. Because we all learned to type as kids and teenagers, we often forget how awkward it was at the beginning. Of course, it seems easy now because you had years of practice. You probably don't even think about your typing process – unless something like an injury incapacitates you. Yet, it wasn't always so easy. So, don't worry if dictation doesn't feel comfortable at first. Eventually, you'll probably get there. But, if you don't, it's not the end of the world.

No one bats an eyelash when an author changes their desk, office chair, or keyboard to make it more comfortable for them to work. Yet, for some reason, we place a sense of shame on people who have tried dictation and not found it as useful as they'd hoped.

Voice recognition software is not for everyone. Let me say it a little louder for the people in the back. There's a chance dictation isn't the tool for you. That's totally okay!

 Have some patience with yourself before you give up. It may take some time for you to feel comfortable verbalizing your story out loud.

There are some steps you can take to help you adapt to the world of dictation.

Take a breath and understand just because it doesn't come naturally in the beginning, doesn't mean that it won't. Even though I have been using voice recognition software more than half my life, using it in a creative environment was a different experience for me. When I started writing fiction, I was excruciatingly slow. If I dictated five hundred words in the day, I felt accomplished. Now, I get five hundred words in about twenty minutes. It's a matter of practice and repetition.

If you are bothered by the sound of your voice, you're not alone. Most of us don't like to hear ourselves talk – especially for hours on end. I recommend noise-canceling headphones to deal with this issue.

Whether you listen to music through them or not is up to you. I like to listen to mellow country music while I dictate because it helps disguise the sound of my voice. I choose music I've heard before so that I don't think about the lyrics too much. I actually have a premium subscription to Pandora so I don't need to listen to commercials. Initially, I was just using the free version However, every time a commercial played, it took me out of my productive headspace. So, it's worth the five dollars a month to me to skip the commercials.

 I play music through my cell phone so I don't disrupt the computer and tax its resources.

Other people swear by programs like Brain FM which play white noise which is supposed to encourage you to be more productive. For me, it had the opposite effect. My brain was trying to figure out what the random sounds were and it made it more difficult for me to dictate. Still, many others report great success when they use white noise. Some people find it helpful to play music that matches the mood of the scene they are writing. If that works for you, go for it!

Dictating punctuation can be daunting to some people. I promise it will get easier.

 Reading existing text and including the punctuation will help you get used to the rhythm and cadence of speaking punctuation out loud. If you take the time to correct the mistakes in your dictation, this can also help train your Dragon® profile to be more accurate.

Eventually, dictating punctuation will probably become so second nature to you that you may have a difficult time leaving voicemails without speaking punctuation marks.

 Speaking slowly or straining your voice to increase your volume is not helpful. It doesn't make Dragon® more accurate. It just has the potential of fatiguing – and potentially damaging – your vocal cords.

Keep your microphone at a consistent distance from your mouth and turn the gain up on your microphone enough that you can speak at a normal speaking voice.

Practice dictating. I mean, it sounds pretty simple. But, dictation is one of those things the more you do it, the better you get. So, there are countless ways every day you can use voice recognition software. You can use the microphone on Google or ask Siri a series of questions. Dragon® works better if it has more context to figure out what you meant to say.

Practice speaking ideas out loud in complete sentences.

In the beginning, it doesn't matter much what you write —just be sure to include punctuation. If you dictate a lot of dialogue, make sure you practice the punctuation patterns present when a character speaks.

It is helpful to use writing prompts to get used to composing creative thoughts as opposed to dictating a list. Some people initially find it difficult to think creatively at the same time they are speaking out loud. These story prompts can be nonsensical. In fact, the harder you think, the more helpful they will be. So, for example, you might ponder what would happen if you were gifted a house in a neighborhood you'd never been to? How would you choose to handle it? If cars had never been invented, how would you design them? What if you had to go back and give your twelve-year-old self advice? Would you listen? If not, why?

You don't have to keep the results of these dictation sessions, although sometimes it's fun to do just to see how far you've come. These writing prompts are just that. They are meant to spur writing – or in our case, the dictation. There are no right or wrong answers, it's about the mechanism of learning to think and dictate at the same time.

This is going to sound counterproductive, but trust me.

 In the beginning, you should completely cover your monitor from time to time. This allows you to get used to the cadence of dictating without worrying about whether you've made mistakes. You will use this skill later if you choose to use transcription.

Sometimes if I get too caught up in trying to edit my work as I write, I will still cover my monitor. This forces me to focus on what I'm saying rather than the corrections I need to make.

Novels Are Built One Word at a Time

You write one word at a time. I know that seems self-evident. Even so, I have encountered many people who believe that as soon as they start dictating, their productivity numbers will skyrocket. For some people that may very well be true. However, for most people learning to dictate is an ongoing process. It's okay to tackle it in small bits.

Every word you dictate brings you closer to success.

Some days, you might be able to dictate thousands of words, other days you might struggle to get a few hundred. Don't let that shake your confidence.

I am not particularly fast at dictation. My cerebral palsy affects my speech when I am sick or fatigued. So, on those days, my accuracy rates fall into the basement. For me, it's a numbers game backed up by the amount of time I spend actually dictating. In my case, the amount of time I spend writing offsets the fact that I'm not a speed demon.

Trust me, over time, the words add up. It just takes patience and practice.

Chapter 9 – What Kind of Writer Are You?

 All approaches to writing are valid. It matters not if you are a plotter, a planser, or a pantser. Each approach has its strengths and weaknesses. It is a matter of playing up the strengths of your personal style and mitigating the weaknesses.

For purposes of discussion, I'm going to discuss writing styles as if they fall into three neat categories. The reality is that your writing style is likely on a continuum. For some projects, you might be more of a plotter than a pantser. On a different project, you might fly by the seat of your pants and write with abandon. Still others you might have a vague idea what you'd like to write, but you haven't written a precise outline. All of these approaches are valid and they all present unique challenges when combined with voice recognition software.

It's Self-Reflection, Not a Contest

I'm going to state this bluntly. I don't care what type of writer you are. One is not better than another. Pick the style which works for you on any given project. Determining which style you are most comfortable with can give you a morale boost. It is easier to write when you are not fighting your natural tendencies. When we talk about determining your default writing style, it is for the purpose of using voice recognition more effectively. There is no "right" writing style.

The Debate Stops Here

All approaches to writing are valid. However, if you're unhappy with the progress you're making as one type of writer, there are any number of books to help you branch out into other styles of writing. This is not that type of guide. I won't try to persuade you to become a certain type of writer. The choice is entirely yours. My job is to give you as many tools as I can to work with your writing style.

Growing Pains

The debate about which type of writing style is best is personal for me. I almost stopped writing before I finished my second book because other authors convinced me that somehow my style was lacking. Eventually, I came to realize I am a dyed-in-the-wool pantser.

The mere mention of the word outline makes me want to break out in a cold sweat. To say I am not a fan of writing outlines is a grotesque understatement. They make me cry. Outlining and briefing is an enormous deal in law school. Everyone is expected to do it. I graduated in the top fifteen percent of my class, but I never got better at outlining.

A few years later, after I'd just published my first book, I was beyond excited. I joined a ton of writing groups, because that's what you do when you want to get better at your job. It is then I discovered the way I wrote my first novel isn't the way it's "supposed" to be done. I wanted to be the strongest author I could possibly be, so I began intensive study into outlining and proper writing craft. I tried everything from the Snowflake method to Save the Cat.

It should have made me a stronger writer, right? Wrong! I was paralyzed with the fear that everything I was writing was wrong and I began to lose confidence. I almost stopped writing completely before my second book was even finished. After all, I was convinced the proper way to write a book was to have an extensive outline. Honestly, the process reduced me to tears. I was unable to write at all until I gave up and gave myself permission to fully embrace my status as a pantser. Once I forgave myself for not being like everyone else, I found my voice again.

That's why it is critically important to me that you feel comfortable with whatever style works for you. I can promise you there are successful authors with every style. You can be one too.

What Style Fits You?

 Authors are rarely completely one type of writer to the exclusion of all others. Most of us adapt our style depending on what we're writing.

Authors are rarely one hundred percent one style and zero percent another. We choose our approach depending on what we're writing. However, it is helpful to understand where your natural tendencies lie. Again, one style is not necessarily better than the other, they just require a different approach when it comes to using voice recognition software.

Whether you are a plotter, a pantser or a planser, you can use dictation to help you write.

Everyone's definitions of a plotter, a planser or a pantser may differ slightly. So, I'll usually review my definition of each style and potential pros and cons of each approach.

Keep in mind, this isn't a debate about the value of leaning toward one writing style over another. These categories are simply tools to help you identify the best way to incorporate dictation into your writing

Plotter

Definition

If you are a plotter, organization is your best friend. You plan out the characters, the story line, the arc, the pacing and the locations with incredible detail. Sticky notes, colored pens and spreadsheets are invaluable tools. You may write long, involved outlines and know each character's back story as well as you know your own. You might even know their personality traits, zodiac signs and ancestry. Descriptions of locations, real or pretend, are determined well in advance and presented meticulously.

You might have a tendency to be a plotter if this sounds like the way you write. That's great news! Voice recognition software can make this process easier.

Pros

Being a plotter can make your stories strong and richly detailed. You can identify and fill plot holes before you even start writing your novel. When you plot, it's easier to understand the overall story arc and the timeline of each character and how they interrelate.

The amount of time you spend working on your outline and research allows you to get to know each and every character on such an intimate level you can plan for fun quirks and traits which make each character unique. You may build an entredentolignumologist's hobby of collecting toothpicks into multiple scenes.

Relationships between your characters can be unusually deep because you have taken the time to learn each character's history and what wounds them or makes them stronger.

Descriptions of locations and weather conditions can be particularly vivid since you've done your research well in advance.

You don't have to stop and interrupt the flow of your writing to look up words, details, names or locations because you've done all the preparation beforehand. By the time you start working on your actual manuscript, you've sorted all the critical details and ironed out any weaknesses in your plan. When you sit down to write your first draft, you have a clear picture of where the story is going and how to get there.

Potential Downside

Plotters can find it frustrating to be focused on all the background material and feel like they'll never start writing the actual story.

While authors who identify themselves as plotters have many strengths to call upon when writing, there are also some potential hurdles for plotters.

First, the process of creating a detailed outline and researching every little detail is time-consuming. It can be frustrating to be focused on all the background material and feel like you'll never start writing the actual story. Sometimes, it's hard to determine how much detail is too much and it can become overwhelming. It is easy to fall down nonproductive rabbit holes and get stuck without any forward motion when you spend a lot of time researching or drafting outlines.

Sometimes, despite our best intentions, characters have a tendency to develop in ways we don't expect during the writing process. If you have done copious amounts of research and outlining, they can be disconcerting when a character doesn't respond the way you anticipated they would. Occasionally, a character or conflict you planned as a minor subplot will assert itself in your story and change your planned focus. As a plotter with a detailed outline, this deviation is frustrating and will send you back to the drawing board.

Some plotters I know who are meticulous plotters become disenchanted with their characters, storyline or plots after working with them extensively. After a while, the storyline begins to feel stale – even if it may not seem that way to readers with fresh eyes.

Finally, applying a method with beats or plot points may not adequately represent the story you want to tell.

Planser

Definition

 If you are a planser, you've learned to exploit the joy of writing by the seat of your pants within the structure of solid preparation. This approach helps move your story forward and avoid gaping potholes.

If you are a planser, you view outlines as merely loose guidelines for where you want your story to go. You may choose major beats you want to hit along the way, but you're not married to your outline. General character sketches and location descriptions are helpful, but it's not the end of the world if your characters deviate from your plan. You try to balance the freewheeling tendency of a pantser against the preparedness of a plotter.

Finding balance is the name of the game for plansers. If this describes your writing style, you've discovered how to leverage the best of both worlds as a planser. I've got great news for you! Voice recognition software can help you make your plans a reality.

Pros

If you are a planser, you've learned to exploit the joy of writing by the seat of your pants within the structure of solid preparation. This approach helps move your story forward and avoid gaping potholes. By having an idea where your story is going, it is easier for you to interweave storylines and introduce secondary characters and subplots. You have a general idea who your characters are and their relative strengths and weaknesses, however if they grow and change throughout the story, you have the flexibility to be able to cope without throwing you off your game. Having a general sense of where the story is going and how to get there gives you a sense of security as you write.

You know how to leverage the strengths of a simple outline while reinforcing your characters free will to direct the story.

Potential Downside

 When you're a planser, it can be tough to determine whether you should wear your plotter hat or your pantser one.

Most of the time, being a planser feels like you are borrowing the strings from each approach and combining them to write a more powerful story. However, it can be hard to find the appropriate balance when you are trying to draw from two types of writing styles. Plansers can find it awkward to not fully identify with either being a plotter or a pantser since the approaches are so diametrically different. Sometimes, it's difficult to determine whether you should wear your plotter hat or your pantser one.

Many of my author friends who are plansers report that it can sometimes be difficult to do organizational tasks when their pantser tendencies are fighting to get to the surface. Conversely, it's hard to completely go with the spirit and fly by the seat of your pants when you are trying to make unruly characters comply with your outline. It can be difficult to feel like you're moving forward with your story when it isn't progressing like you'd planned.

Pantser

Definition

 If someone asks you what's going to happen in your novel and you answer that you'll get back to them after you write it, you're probably a pantser.

If you rub your hands together with glee when an idea hits and you open a blank document, you might be a pantser. If someone asks you what your story is about and you answer that you have no clue until after you write it, you are most definitely a pantser. This colloquial term comes from the phrase fly by the seat of your pants. It refers to character directed storytelling. Often, authors who write in this style literally have no idea what the outcome will be until after they've written their stories. Pantsing is often an exhilarating, scary way to tell a story. Yet many authors, me included, love this approach because we get as much joy out of discovering the story during the writing process as readers do.

If this sounds like your writing style, I've got great news for you. Voice recognition software can help your stories fly high.

Pros

Pantsing your way through a story and coming out with a strong cohesive story in the end is one of the most exhilarating feelings in the world. Letting your characters direct the story through their eyes can be incredibly realistic. Dialogue unfolds naturally and the reader sees the world through the eyes of the character as if they are in the character's shoes. This style of writing can often highlight strong emotions and relationships feel authentic and true to life.

Stories can feel less formulaic since they don't follow a prescribed path. Characters and storylines don't grow stale because each plot development is fresh and new as the author memorializes each event. Authors who write by the seat of their pants often say it sometimes feels like they are simply writing up incident reports about someone else's life. Pantsers often speak in terms of characters talking to us. Our characters feel like our friends as we watch them complete unexpected journeys.

Pantsers can capture the excitement of a new story without having to pause and write an outline. They can focus on capturing moments in time rather than the process of outlining. This approach can create a dynamic story with deep emotion and exciting conflict.

Potential Downside

When you're a pantser, characters with different agendas can lead to conflicting storylines and create plot holes which are difficult to fix.

Pantsing can be an exhilarating way to create stories. If everything is working well, stories written with this method can be wildly creative. However, it doesn't always go well and when a pantser's story goes off the rails, it can be like watching a train wreck.

Sometimes, characters can take you in a direction which leads to conflicting information and huge plot holes. Not every story arc or plot point developed along the way should be kept in the story. When this happens, it is difficult to cull the words you've worked so diligently to create.

If you have a strong sense of the characters and their conflicts, pantsing can be remarkably effective. However, if you lose focus on your character or have too many characters, it can cause you to drop a storyline that should run throughout the story.

Characters with different agendas can lead to conflicting storylines and create plot holes which are difficult to fix. Because your story is created on the fly, it can be susceptible to changes in your mood or personal circumstances. Over time, it can be difficult to keep characters true to their personalities and temperament.

The time you save by not doing extensive research and outlining can be easily eaten up by the additional editing you may need to do if you discover inconsistent storylines, incomplete story arcs, or plot points with poor pacing and inconsistent conflict.

Many pantsers report that adequately creating tension and conflict is difficult when you don't plan for it in advance.

Lastly, when you write by the seat of your pants, there is a temptation to include multiple complex storylines which may conflict with each other and obscure the main plot and characters.

Now that I've defined all the writing styles and given you an overview of the strengths and weaknesses of each approach, we are ready to move on to the best way to introduce dictation to your specific writing style. Be sure to read through each writing style, even if it does not match your own because there are hidden gems in each section which you may find helpful – regardless of which style of writing you prefer.

Chapter 10 – Give Me a Plan and Make It Detailed

Plotting to Prevail

As a plotter, you need tools to help you get and stay organized. Fortunately, voice-recognition software works well with many of these programs.

As an author, my life got exponentially easier when I discovered I could drag my folders under favorites in the Finder. No more searching my hard drive to figure out where I put critical information and manuscripts. Each story has its own folder under favorites. Within that folder, I typically add a file for graphics.

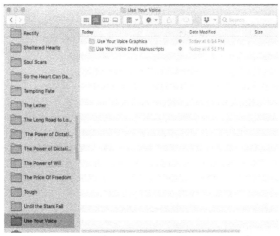

Figure 17: File Organization in Finder

After you've decided where to put your files, the next choice is which program you're going to use to create them.

Scrivener is my first choice for this task, however if Scrivener is not your thing, there are other options. If I was working with Microsoft products, I would probably start with OneNote. This product from Microsoft allows you to collect things in one spot – like the research folder within Scrivener. You can add pictures, texts, websites, PDFs and other documents. OneNote is web-based and readily accessible from multiple computers if you have Wi-Fi access. If you write sensitive material or you want to keep a pen name private, you can assign passwords to certain sections. OneNote is standard on the Mac version of Office 365. If you are using it on the Windows platform, it may be a separate download, depending on which version you are using.

Interestingly enough, OneNote was fully compatible with Dragon® Professional Individual 6.0.8. However, things got a little more complicated on the Windows side when I tried to use it with Dragon® Professional Individual 15.3.

Initially, I couldn't get Dragon® to work with OneNote. However, after I deleted my version of Office 365 and re-downloaded it, it worked just fine. So, if you have trouble dictating directly into Microsoft products, you might want to try reinstalling your Office.

Figure 18: Organization Example Using OneNote

Scrivener is uniquely suited for plotters because it allows you to easily organize your documents into scenes and plot points. You can drag them around and move them into different places without having to copy and paste. Additionally, you can add websites, music clips, manipulate external files such as databases, Excel documents, and even calendars, with the help of bookmarks.

Scrivener creates index cards, and an outline. If you like to outline, you can start there and everything you write in the outline will be transferred to your binder and to your index cards on the cork board. Conversely, if index cards really light your fire, you can plot your whole book out in the cork board mode and the information will be placed in both your outline and your binder.

Figure 19: Organizational Structure Utilizing Scrivener 3 for Mac

There are several templates available for Scrivener which already have hot points built in. For example, one of my favorite beat sheet templates is *Romancing the Beat* by Gwen Haynes which she provides for free on her website to accompany her book by the same title.

Romancing the Beat Link:
(http://gwenhayes.com/free-stuff/romancing_the_beat/)

There are also templates available for the *Snowflake Method*, *Save the Cat* and the *Hero's Journey*. If you are stumped for organizational ideas or want to try a new approach, I would urge you to download some of these templates and see if you can find one that fits your writing style and personality.

Of course, there are Microsoft Word templates available as well. A brief Internet search came up with several customizable options which follow many different types of outline structures and beat sheets.

When downloading templates or other forms from the Internet, make sure your virus protection is turned on and fully operational.

You may want to use an Excel spreadsheet to help build your story bible or expand on your outline. Many others I know use spreadsheets to keep track of complex plot points and character sketches. This preparation will serve you well as you dictate. You can dictate directly into Excel with either version of Dragon® Professional Individual. After you have created a spreadsheet in Excel, you can link it to your document with a bookmark. A bookmark will allow you to edit your spreadsheet on the fly without having to reimport it into your document.

There is some advanced prep you can do to help Dragon® work more effectively.

Advanced Prep

One of the first things you can do to help Dragon® help you is to add custom vocabulary words. I use this feature for adding complex names. For example, I have a recurring character in my series called Darya. However, whenever I attempted to simply dictate Darya, Dragon® routinely misunderstood me and wrote Darius. Finally, I added Darya with a custom pronunciation. Whenever I need the name Darya to appear, I simply say, "character Darya". The same is true for my character Kennadie. It didn't matter how many times I added the unique spelling to my list of custom words, Kennadie was always the second or third option. So, I added an alternative pronunciation "baby Kennadie". Now, Dragon® knows exactly what I want when I use the custom pronunciation.

 If you are adding words to the custom vocabulary list in Dragon® Professional Individual 6.0.8, you need to add the words first and save your profile.

Adding your character's first and last name together as well is in the possessive form will speed things up. If you have unusual locations, you may want to add them as well. The Vocabulary Editor is helpful because it allows you to add alternative pronunciations. Also, if you have experience with dictation and you know there are words which are problematic for you, you can add them in advance. For example, Dragon® very rarely ever recognizes the word mirror when I dictate. So, I added mirror with the alternative pronunciation which approximates what it sounds like when I say the word.

If your writing style involves using curse words, you may want to add them to the custom vocabulary list in advance.

You can train your custom words in your own voice. However, one word of caution if you are adding words to the custom vocabulary list in Dragon® Professional Individual 6.0.8, you need to add the words first and save your profile. Then, you can go back and train each individual word you have added. Don't try to do this at the same time because it will likely cause your computer to crash.

If you use the Mac version, you will have to add custom pronunciations of your words one at a time. There is no mechanism on the Mac side to add vocabulary words with alternative pronunciations in bulk. That's not to say you can't use vocabulary training to feed your computer a document with all the names and locations listed, including possessive forms. If you have another book in the series with the same characters, it would be a gold mine of information to use with Voice Training. However, make sure it is checked thoroughly for errors before you feed it into the vocabulary training tool. Otherwise, you could be teaching Dragon® to make mistakes.

If your writing style involves using curse words, you may want to add them to the custom vocabulary list in advance. Understandably, Dragon® has a bias against making cuss words the default option. In most business headings, this isn't appropriate. However, for writing fiction, it may be. So, simply add custom vocabulary words by editing your vocabulary. Anecdotally, I have noticed that words I give a custom pronunciation to tend to appear more reliably as the first option in my dictation.

If you are using Dragon® Professional Individual 15.3, and you need to import a large list of characters or other custom words, the process can be done in bulk.

To create a list of custom words and phrases manually in Dragon® NaturallySpeaking:
   a. Launch a word processor or notepad and create a new blank document.
   b. On the first line of the document, type: @version=Plato-UTF8
   c. Beginning on the next line, type a word or phrase you want to import. This will be the

written form in Dragon®. If you want a different spoken form, type two backslashes after the written form and then type the spoken form. For example, for the entry below, Dragon® will write Darya when you say "character Darya": Darya\\ character Darya

d. Enter a line break and type the rest of the words and phrases, making sure to start each entry on a new line. It is important to make sure each custom vocabulary word has its own individual line.

e. Save the document as a TXT file.

After you have added your custom words, you can feed documents with a similar feel and voice to the vocabulary trainer. It's important to choose samples which are representative of the writing style in your current work in progress. For example, if you usually write steamy romance, you probably don't want to use samples of your hot romance to teach Dragon® to adapt itself to your voice and cadence if your next few projects are going to be clean and wholesome, middle grade novels.

Under extreme circumstances, I've seen authors use completely different custom vocabulary words and profiles for their different approaches to writing. Dragon® is so accurate right out of the box, there is some debate about whether having completely separate profiles really makes a difference.

Another step in your preparation is to create whatever supporting documents you need – Excel spreadsheets, databases, PDFs whatever you might refer to in fleshing out your outline.

In Scrivener, minimize your window so you have some room on your desktop. Then, choose the Excel file you want and drag it to the bookmark area (circled in red in the following Figure).

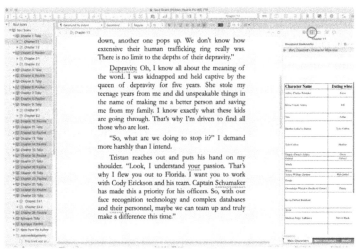

Figure 20: Adding a Bookmark to an External Document in Scrivener 3

If you choose this method instead of importing your Excel spreadsheet, you can make edits by clicking on the bookmark. If you import a file, it is merely a snapshot at the time you saved the file.

Scrivener is one of those programs which works differently on each platform. Dragon® Professional Individual 6.0.8 works beautifully with Scrivener 3 with full correction and editing capabilities.

Unfortunately, Scrivener for Windows is a little more complicated.

Although you can technically dictate into Scrivener, when you do so, you don't have full text control and it is difficult to correct your mistakes or edit your work. So, in order to use Dragon® Professional Individual 15.3 most effectively with Scrivener for Windows, you need to dictate into another application first and copy and paste.

It might be tempting to use the Dragon®Pad, but please don't because it is prone to crashing and will take everything you dictated with it.

My favorite replacement for Dragon®Pad is Speech Productivity Pro. It is everything Dragon®Pad was meant to be and more. Most importantly, it automatically backs up your work so that even if Dragon® crashes, your words are safe and sound.

However, if you don't want the added expense of an add-on program, Notepad, WordPad, OneNote and Text Edit work just fine.

Once you have completed your outline and other background material, I recommend printing it out and putting it in a notebook. Although you can technically read off the screen as you dictate, unless you have multiple monitors, it is easier to read off the printed page.

Tips for Success

In many ways, plotters have an advantage over other approaches to writing when using dictation. The accuracy of voice recognition software increases when you speak in long sentences.

 Dragon®'s software is based on artificial intelligence which predicts your next word based on the words you said before. So, if you can dictate in full complete thoughts, Dragon® has a better chance of guessing what you meant to say correctly.

For example, ice cream and I scream sound the same when you dictate them, the context surrounding those words lets Dragon® know which phrase you meant to say.

As a plotter, you may find it helpful to have your outline in front of you while you dictate. You can include key pieces of dialogue or special phrasing in your outline. A report cover (like the ones used in school) can be helpful to organize your outline, plot points and other reference material. Additionally, if you easily lose your place in your outline or spreadsheet, you can make a masking card out of poster board. Just take a piece of light weight cardboard (I prefer to use a dark color, but the choice is yours) and cut it to slightly wider than your reading material. Then with an X-Acto knife cut out a window which is wide enough for you to read a small chunk of your text at a time. Then, as you dictate pieces of your outline, just move the reading mask down to the next level. This helps ensure you don't repeat material you've already covered.

If Dragon® has a difficult time recognizing one of your custom names or locations, you can add another version to your custom words with an alternative form of pronunciation. Additionally, if an existing vocabulary word within Dragon® is giving you fits, you can train each individual word and give it a custom pronunciation if you wish. I had to do this with the words mirror and succinct.

If you deviate from your outline, you can always turn the text a different color or highlight it so you can locate it quickly, in case the new direction has ramifications for the rest of the plot line or character development.

If you are dictating and your character deviates from the outline and goes rogue, feel free to continue working. You can mark the text a different color or highlight it. I learned this trick the hard way when I changed the occupation of a character in the middle of my story. I forgot to make note of it and it caused issues during editing.

Another way to deal with this problem is to link your outline to your document and edit it in real time.

Remember voice activation software works better in smaller documents. There is less lag time especially when you are using Microsoft Word. Later, you can combine scenes if you need to. If I'm working in Microsoft Word, I try to keep each section to less than two thousand words.

Remember, you can use various views within Scrivener or even Microsoft Word to see the structure of your document. In Scrivener, if you make changes in one area, it changes the output in every view. So, no copying and pasting is required.

 Regardless of which version of Scrivener you use, you can only have your file open in one location at a time. If you want to use the IOS version, make sure the file is not already open on your computer.

If you like to dictate on your iPhone or iPad, Scrivener has an IOS version. It is less full-featured than either the Mac or Windows version. However, it is quite functional and a good option when you want to take your structure with you. When I use the IOS version of Scrivener, I dictate into Dragon® Anywhere and copy and paste it into my Scrivener document.

A word of caution about using the IOS version of Scrivener. Keep the number of projects in your app folder small because it takes a while to sync. Only one version of your project can be open at the same time. So, if you move from your computer to your phone, you need to make sure the file on your Mac or Windows computer is closed first. It is best to sync with your phone or iPad where you have reliable, fast Wi-Fi access. The process can take a while. Make sure you save your file when you exit the mobile version.

As always, I recommend you save your files in multiple locations in case of catastrophic failure. Even though most applications like Scrivener, Microsoft Office and Open Office have automatic backup features, sometimes they fail. After I lost a significant chunk of about fifteen thousand words because of a computer malfunction with Scrivener, I began compiling a copy of my manuscript every day and sending it to myself on Facebook.

If plotting is your jam, rock on! I, for one, am impressed. I hope you found tips helpful and your productivity will increase exponentially. However, not everyone is a plotter. Some authors like to take a more moderate approach to preparation. I call these people plansers. Next, I'll discuss strategies to successfully use dictation as a planser.

Chapter 11 – Milestones Are Great, But I May Wander

Planning for Victory

If you enjoy the freedom of flying by the seat of your pants, but need the security of a roadmap, plansing may be right up your alley. Integrating voice recognition software into this style of writing can make a world of difference.

A planser borrows the best of both worlds and makes them work together. There are many applications out there to help with this process. Evernote has a few great ones on their site for free. You can sign up for a free Evernote account and sync your documents across platforms. It works for Mac, Windows, iOS, and Android. You can upgrade to the premium version for six dollars a month and have the ability to email your account. In addition, Dragon® Anywhere syncs directly with Evernote.

If you are a fan of Scrivener, you can drag links to your Evernote notebooks into the research portion of your project and edit them while you're working. By the way, the same approach can be taken with your notes in OneNote, if you wish. Simply choose the share option and copy and paste the URL. Place the URL in your browser and then drag it to the research simple novel outlines for Microsoft Word section of the binder in your project.

If you prefer to write and outline in Microsoft Word, Stef Mcdaid has made a wonderful web tutorial on her website Write Into Print about how to effectively format your writing up front so that uploading to Amazon is less troublesome. http://www.writeintoprint.com/p/layout-tips.html

One of the challenges when you are a Planser is doing enough advanced planning that it's helpful without becoming overwhelming. Dabble has a tool with a very simple interface which you might find helpful.

Advanced Prep

If you need to add a large list of words to Dragon Professional Individual 6.0.8, you can add them using the Vocabulary Trainer.

There is some preparation you can do with Dragon® Professional Individual before you start writing as a planser. Primarily, you need to add any custom vocabulary words to Dragon®. If you are using Dragon® Professional Individual 6.0.8, you have to do this one at a time or use vocabulary training with a document which contains all of your specialized terminology.

Dragon® Professional Individual 15.3 for Windows provides a special mechanism to upload words to the custom vocabulary in bulk.

When you are adding character names, businesses and locations, don't forget to add any custom usage of words.

For example, in one of my series, the characters use clean versions of cuss words. In that book, Soufflé, French Toast and Oh Hershey's Bars are common expressions. In some of my books, I feature a recurring character with Tourette's syndrome. I indicate his verbal tic with jigger, jig, jig. So, I added an entry in my custom vocabulary words with an alternate pronunciation. When I say "jigger phrase", jigger, jig, jig appears.

Tips for Success

As a Planser, your outline will be less comprehensive than if you were a full plotter. Still, it is a good idea to print out your outline materials so you can refer to them when you dictate. The levels of your outline may be more general than someone who uses the Snowflake method, for example. However, that doesn't mean having a roadmap isn't helpful when you are dictating. Knowing where you're headed may help you speak in longer, more comprehensive sentences.

Because you are giving your characters freer reign, your outline is susceptible to change. So, it is a good idea to either keep your outline open or put a bookmark in the program you are using so you can reference it as a live document and make changes on the fly.

Making changes to your story structure is incredibly easy in Scrivener. You can add and subtract sections at will and move them around if they don't fit well where you originally put them.

It is not quite as easy to move sections around in Microsoft Word however, the program does have an overall view which works well if you are applying styles as you write.

Part of the joy of being a planser is letting your creativity flow and writing what comes naturally.

You can add your plot guideposts to the notes in your Scrivener file so you generally know where you would like to end up.

Although I am a diehard pantser, I have begun inching my way toward being a planser. I still start with a blank page when it comes to the storyline. Generally speaking, all I know about my story is the characters' names. However, recently, I have incorporated the *Romancing the Beat* plot points into my blank novel template in Scrivener. I don't follow them prescriptively, still they give me an idea of what I should highlight at any given time in my story.

If you change details in your story which don't follow your rough outline, you need to mark that somehow so that it is easier to find the changes when you are editing your first draft. You can do that by bookmarking the area, writing in a different font color or using the highlight tool.

With a little advanced preparation, the plansing writing style works well with dictation. Even so, some authors feel more comfortable discovering the story as they go along and prefer not to have the constraints of predetermined structure. These people truly like to fly by the seat-of-their-pants. Voice recognition software can be a valuable tool for pantsers as well.

Chapter 12 – Plan? I Don't Need No Stinkin' Plan

Flying by the Seat of Your Pants

If the sight of a blank page makes your day, you're probably a pantser. There is a persistent rumor among authors which states you can't effectively dictate if you write by the seat of your pants.

Respectfully, I disagree. How do I know you do not need a detailed outline to use dictation? I've written thirty-two books using voice recognition software. I've written all of them as a pantser. As I shared before, I tried to adapt my style to what I thought "real" authors expected. That strategy was a complete and total bust.

It is not only possible to write compelling novels using voice recognition software, sometimes not having a plan frees you up to dictate faster.

Even though as a pantser you may not have a formal outline, there is still some advanced prep you can elect to do to make your experience more successful.

Advanced Prep

 Pause for a moment before you begin speaking to formulate your thought. Try to speak in complete sentences as this helps Dragon® more precisely choose which words to use in context.

Pantsing is a unique style of writing. It has a different cadence to it. You may stop and start more often than if you were reading from an outline. This can have a detrimental effect on your accuracy rate. Therefore, it is advisable to pause for a moment before you begin speaking to formulate your thought. Try to speak in complete sentences, as this helps Dragon® more precisely choose which words to use in context.

Authors have different approaches to pantsing. Some, like me, typically know the names of the characters and the locations of the stories. I have two long-running series. So, when I start a new book, I don't need to add very many characters to my custom vocabulary. I generally know the names of the main characters in advance. I add those to my custom vocabulary words before I start dictating. I add their first and last names as well as possessive forms like Tayanita Moya's to the custom vocabulary list. This helps cut down on recognition errors. The same is true for any known locations.

If you don't know this information up front, it's not a huge deal. You can add character names or location names as you go along. Alternatively, you can use simpler names and use the find and replace feature at the end of your dictation. I often use Sally and Travis because it is easy for me to say and Dragon® does not misunderstand those names. However, sometimes generic names can create a stumbling block to your creativity. In that case, I suggest adding the character names with custom pronunciations.

If you are having difficulty with accuracy, you can choose to use vocabulary training to familiarize Dragon®'s speech models with your particular writing style. If you choose this option, make sure your writing sample is free of spelling and grammatical errors.

Another way to improve Dragon®'s chances of recognizing your speech correctly is to train it with samples of your own writing.

This form of training involves reading works you have already done out loud. Make sure you fix any recognition errors. As I've stated before, correcting your mistakes is more effective in Dragon® Professional Individual 15.3 than it is in Dragon® Professional Individual 6.0.8. Even so, under the circumstances I would take the time to correct any mis-recognition errors, even in the Mac version.

Staring at a blank page can be daunting for any author, but with some simple strategies, you can conquer the challenges of pantsing and successfully use voice recognition software.

Tips for Success

I can't stress this enough - so I'm going to say it again. Even if you don't have a formal plan in mind as you write, it is important to try to string together several words in a row. Technically, Dragon® can still recognize your speech if you dictate one word at a time. However, your accuracy rate will soar if you dictate in full sentences or paragraphs.

So, how do you do that if you don't know exactly what you're going to write? When I dictate, I try to compose my thought before I verbalize it. So, if you were to listen to me dictate, there are a lot of pauses between my sentences as I mentally construct my thought before speaking. Of course, sometimes you'll change your mind in the middle or thoughts won't come fluently.

I combat my tendency to edit as I speak by writing with a self-imposed deadline. I am a huge fan of sprinting. Writing against a specific timeframe helps ensure that I have my creative hat on and my editing hat off. I simply don't have time to go back and reword something when I am sprinting. That is not to say I don't edit my first, second, and third draft. It just means I don't do it in the middle of my writing process. Although I typically like to write for fifty minutes in a single sprinting session, when I start for the day, I complete a couple of shorter sprints to get into the flow of things.

As my back catalog has grown, I've become more consistent in terms of my voice and my pacing. Now, my books follow a general template of twenty-four to twenty-six chapters. In my novel template in Scrivener, I mark the chapter I believe will be the midpoint of my novels or novellas. This helps keep me on track and make sure my book is not unbalanced. Additionally, I use story beats by Gwen Hayes as outlined in Romancing the Beat. While I don't follow the beats religiously, they give me a good idea of what tension points I need to reach in each section.

Other than that, I start with just character names and general locations. The rest of it is a blank canvas. I try not to edit as I write. Instead, I read my material the next morning. If a scene is sending my characters on a weird tangent, I don't completely discard the scene. I simply move the scene to a folder in the research section of my binder. Although the scene may not fit where I originally wrote it, the material may work somewhere else. Never throw way your words.

If you are tempted to stop and research while you are dictating, you can break yourself of that habit by using square brackets.

If you are tempted to stop and research while you are dictating, you can break yourself of that habit by using square brackets. I place everything I need to change or research in square brackets. For example, if I find myself using a particular phrase I know I overuse and need to change to more specific language, I will place it in square brackets. The same goes for research. For example, I don't drink. Any time my characters choose a wine for a special occasion, I need to research because it is outside of my frame of reference. So, if my characters go on a picnic and they have wine and fancy cheese, I would put [wine and fancy cheese] in square brackets to know that when I take a break from dictating, I can search for the appropriate kind of wine and cheese to take on a picnic.

After you have dictated several scenes in your new work in progress, you can correct it for spelling errors and grammar mistakes, and run it through Vocabulary Training. This tool will find words you don't already have in your custom dictionary. Incidentally, this tool can help you identify misspelled words you may have missed in your manuscript.

Regardless of which writing style you have or which version of Dragon® Professional Individual you use, you will have to deal with some of the idiosyncrasies which can pop up when you use voice recognition software. In the next section, I will discuss how to cope with some of those oddities so they don't affect your final manuscript.

Chapter 13 – Correcting, Editing and Cleaning Up

Homophones and Other Common Errors

A homophone is when you type one word but you meant to use another word which sounds the same but is spelled differently. These types of errors occur when you use voice recognition software. It is inevitable because machine logic can't always tell the proper meaning. Generally speaking, if you dictate in longer sentences, Dragon® has a better shot at guessing the correct word for the context. However, it is prone to making mistakes with their, there, and they're, as well as to, two, and too. I don't know if it's the way I pronounce things, but

Dragon® has an extremely difficult time determining whether I say error or air. This is also true for mere and mirror.

The best way to combat this deficiency is to dictate in complete sentences, so Dragon® can determine which version of the word you intend to use. However, even this is not foolproof. Over time you can get a better sense of which words Dragon® is likely to misrecognize in your own speech patterns and keep an eye out for them when you edit your work.

In addition to homophones, Dragon® can mishear words. If you're like me and you have a slight speech impediment, there may be more errors. There are words Dragon® consistently gets wrong for me. This list might be different for you. I have to watch out for then and than, is and isn't, can and can't, that's and what's.

Sometimes the issue is punctuation, as in the words let's and lets, or its or it's. I haven't come up with a great solution for this other than careful editing.

Occasionally (Okay, I'll be honest here – some days, it's more than just occasionally), the mistake will be mine. On days I am really tired, I tend to forget to dictate the closing quotation marks. I know it's hard when you're facing down deadlines, but sometimes you need to rest to save your productivity.

I actually have two profiles. I have one specifically set up for when I have upper respiratory issues which impact the quality of my dictation. If your dictation sounds different in different environments or when your health is challenged, this might be a viable solution for you too.

Spacing Issues

Dragon® has a habit of placing an extra space before each word. In most cases, this is a helpful programming feature however, when it occurs at the beginning of paragraphs or after you've made a correction, it can be annoying. So, after you finish dictating your first draft, you can easily fix these spacing issues with find and replace.

Both versions of Dragon® Professional Individual have a habit of leaving a leading space before you dictate something. Additionally, if you correct something in Dragon® Professional Individual 6.0.8, the program sometimes adds spaces around the text you just corrected. It is important to edit these spaces out before you publish your manuscript. Fortunately, I've developed some easy methods to accomplish this.

In Scrivener, the spacing problem is best dealt with in Project Replace. To accomplish this task, you need to make sure your invisibles are on. First, copy a ¶ into your clipboard. Then click on the Project Replace button.

Paste the ¶ into the top box and press the space bar once.

Go to the bottom box and paste the ¶ again but do not press the space bar this time.

Now, press the Replace button. The program will give you a warning which will make you think you are about to plan the apocalypse, but it's fine – all you're doing is removing extra spaces. It's like magic! The leading spaces should be gone. You may have to run this check more than once. If the extra space is before the first word in a chapter or section, you'll need to remove the leading space by hand.

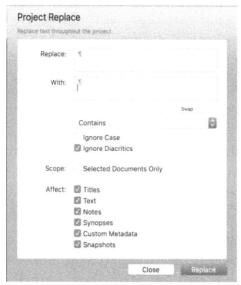

Figure 21: Removing Spaces before Paragraphs in Scrivener

In Microsoft Word, the process is similar, but the vernacular is different. For Word, you need to use Find and Replace. In the top box, type ^p and then press the space bar. In the bottom box, type ^p. Click Replace All.

All the leading spaces should now be gone.

Figure 22: Removing Spaces before Paragraphs in Word

Removing double spaces follows the same concept. In Scrivener, go to Project Replace and type two spaces in the top box and one space in the bottom box, then click the Replace button. You may need to repeat this function more than once. Just continue to do it until it says not found.

In Microsoft Word, use the Find and Replace function to remove extra spaces. In the top box, type two spaces and in the bottom box, type only one space. Click Replace All. This should resolve the issue.

If you are using Dragon® Professional Individual 6.0.8, you may have an additional problem with what I affectionately call Dragon®

poop. These extra characters and numbers in your document can wreak havoc and cause you a great deal of stress. However, there are some simple ways to minimize the impact of this Dragon® glitch.

Racing Cursors and Dragon® Poop

You have a Mac. Congratulations! Dragon® Professional Individual 6.0.8 is all loaded, prepped and ready to go on your computer. Great! Just understand there are a few glitches which can drive you a little nuts.

Your Dragon® will crash.

It's not the end of the world.

Dragon® Dictate will likely at some point leave behind what I affectionately call Dragon poop. Dragon poop most often consists of letters, but sometimes numbers or random punctuation left behind after it's lost its place in your document.

Don't panic!

Because of the way Apple writes its code, Dragon Professional Individual 6.0.8 has a problem keeping track of where it is in your document. This is often exacerbated if you use your keyboard to input information while you are dictating. Dragon®

keeps a cache of information about your document in its history to assist with editing. If you input information via your keyboard or mouse, it disrupts this record-keeping and can make the program lose its place, causing the cursor to race around your document looking for words it can't find. I recommend you refrain from touching your keyboard or mouse while you are dictating. I understand breaking away from using your keyboard is very difficult. I struggle with this too. I've begun wearing sweatshirts with a large pocket in the front where I place my hands while I dictate to dissuade me from using my keyboard. It's a subtle reminder to not type while I am in the process of dictating.

If Dragon® misrecognizes a command, it can cause the same problems. Try to enunciate your commands quite clearly, especially commands which end in the word that.

If this happens and you see your cursor racing up the screen, simply wait for it to stop. If you see it delete a word, you can press COMMAND + Z to restore the deleted text. Additionally, the program may leave behind some random letters, numbers or punctuation when you try to dictate your next few words. (It is this unfortunate side effect I refer to as Dragon® poop.) If this occurs, simply backspace and delete those characters. The next step is to say Cache Document. This will empty out the cache and reset it. It will eliminate the extra characters which are appearing after your sentences.

The other circumstance which often causes your cursor to race through your document is if you say Correct That and Dragon misunderstands what you meant. Sometimes, it will look for the word that. If you make a correction by voice, I suggest using Correct < misrecognized word>.

Although Dragon Professional Individual 6.0.8 is relatively stable in almost all applications, if you have difficulty with Dragon® crashing often, make sure you have the most recent version. The most recent version of Dragon® Professional Individual for Mac is 6.0.8. The difference between Dragon® Professional Individual 6.0 and 6.0.8 cannot be emphasized enough. This is one piece of software you absolutely, positively need to make sure you update. Even though Nuance® has stopped selling Dragon Professional Individual 6.0.8, they have pledged to keep their knowledge base available to Mac users. This includes the update to 6.0.8 which is available here:

http://Nuance®.custhelp.com/app/answers/detail/a_id/26574/~/information-on-dragon-professional-individual-for-mac-6.0.8

Dragon® functions better if there are very few other programs running, especially big programs like Microsoft Word or Photoshop. If I dictate in Microsoft Word, I keep my file size very small.

In the event Dragon Professional Individual 6.0.8 has a meltdown, you are not likely to lose any information – unless you've disregarded my advice and elected to use Dragon®Pad. Once again, please don't use Dragon®Pad. If you are using Dragon® Pad and Dragon crashes, you will lose everything. My recommendation is to use a program like Grammarly, Notes or Scrivener 3, which back up automatically.

If Dragon Professional Individual 6.0.8 crashes, you do not need to close down the system completely. Simply start up your Activity Monitor, which is a utility that comes standard with the Mac OS. I use it often enough I placed the Activity Monitor on my toolbar. If your Dragon® program becomes unresponsive, simply open the Activity Monitor and click on the CPU button. If Dragon® is frozen up, the application should be highlighted in red. Select it. Then click Quit and then Force Quit in the next window. This will completely close down Dragon Professional Individual 6.0.8. You'll have to restart your application. However, this will not disturb any other applications you may have running.

Chapter 14 – That's All She Wrote

If you don't plant your butt in front of a microphone and talk, the words won't magically appear. Trust me, I wish I could just think about stories and have them show up for me to publish. Unfortunately, it doesn't work that way.

I know I have thrown an incredible amount of information at you. You may be feeling completely overwhelmed. That's okay. Most people who are not facing injury or illness which prevents them from typing can ease into dictating. Learning to dictate takes lots of practice and patience. Let me emphasize that dictating doesn't feel natural for most people. Then again, you weren't born with the knowledge of how to type on a computer either. You had to take the time to master the skill. So, give yourself some grace if dictation doesn't come naturally.

I imagine some of you are saying that I make it sound too easy and too good to be true. It hasn't been all smooth sailing. I wrote this book so that you could avoid making some of the mistakes I've made. If the advice in this book has a ring of truth to it it's because I have struggled with voice recognition software for a long time. Even though I have lots of experience using dictation, using it in a creative fashion was a new experience for me. Honestly, some days are better than others. Occasionally, I feel like I delete more things than I keep. I suspect it's probably the same for people who type. But since I don't really type, I don't know that for sure.

I'm not a person who hides the ball. If I have a tip which will help you become a better author, you are welcome to it. Having said that, what works for me may not work for someone else.

The other reason I wrote this book was to help end the stigma about different writing styles. Just as we all bring different voices to our books, we all have our own individual ways of writing. However you write, it's fine. If you want to change and move toward a different style of writing, that's okay too. Even though I am a very proud pantser, over time I have moved on the spectrum toward being a planser because I have discovered tools which work for me. Don't feel like you have to stick to one style of writing for everything you write. Choose whatever style fits the project.

I've learned some lessons the hard way. If I had learned them earlier, I could've saved myself a great deal of money. When it comes to computers, it is better to err on the side of too much power then not enough. I know computers are expensive. However, they are tools of the trade and you need to invest in your success – particularly if you are going to use voice recognition software. The hardware you use matters. Don't be like me and try to skimp to save money. In the long run, I've cost myself a bunch.

The other lesson I've learned the hard way is to pay attention to not only the quality of the microphone you purchased but the form. I can't tell you how many headsets I've purchased over the last thirty years in hopes they wouldn't drive me crazy. Because I wear glasses, wearing headsets frustrates me. They never seem to stay where I put them. When I discovered the Yeti by Blue Mic, I found the accuracy was nothing short of miraculous. You can get high quality mics for much less than they used to cost. Go to a knowledgeable source like Knowbrainer.com and look at the actual accuracy reviews before you choose a microphone. The best mic for you may not be the same as it is for someone else.

Pick the writing software program which works for what you need. I write long books – some of them are over one hundred thousand words. So, Microsoft Word couldn't cope very well with the demands I placed on it. For me, trying Scrivener was an eye-opening experience. Finally, I could visualize the structure of my document and put all the resources I collect along the way in one place. It changed the way I approach writing. I love Scrivener so much I own it for Mac, Windows and iOS.

 National Novel Writing Month (NaNoWriMo) was a game changer for me. It taught me the art of writing quickly and ignoring your inner critic during the writing process.

The goal of NaNoWriMo is to write fifty-thousand words in a month. I now basically NaNoWriMo every single month when I am healthy. Sometimes, it's good to move out of your comfort zone.

When I first started writing creatively, it was a stretch for me to write five hundred words a day. Now, I can do that in just a few minutes. I am not a particularly fast dictator. Instead, I am persistent. I dictate many hours every day seven days a week. You will get faster the more you practice. It helps me to envision my characters as real people. If I am writing a high tension argument, I try to put myself in the shoes of each character.

Accountability is a strong motivator. I use an app called Pacemaker Press to keep track of my projects and to manage my daily word counts. Together with sprinting, I am able to stay on track. When I need to, I block social media sites with an app called Focus.

You can't publish what you don't write. I know that sounds simplistic. But it's true. Even if your first draft is rough, you can edit it. If you are so focused on getting everything perfect as you write it, you become frozen with fear. Don't let perfection be the enemy of progress.

It's okay to make mistakes. It happens and you can always improve what you've written. I've recently reedited every book in my back catalog because I have become a stronger author over the past five years. Since I knew better, I was able to fix some of my deficient writing and editing.

It's okay to use tools to write. It doesn't make it any less organic or real. It just makes it easier for readers to relate to what you've written. My favorite editing application is ProWritingAid because it allows you to edit directly into your Scrivener or Word document. I am so consistent in my writing that I make the same errors in every book. Consequently, I have developed a list of words that I pre-edit for. I do this before my beta readers even see my work. These words include so, pretty, really, that, just, to me, start to, begin to and going to. Pre-editing for these words saves me time when I run ProWritingAid.

In my opinion, ProWritingAid is a more comprehensive grammar and spell checker than Grammarly. Having said that, I still use Grammarly on a daily basis. I use it like a fancy clipboard. Since it backs up all your files to the web, it is easy to make notes and write social media posts.

Writing gets easier with time. You develop tools which work for you. For example, I have both a fiction and a nonfiction template I use in Scrivener. That means my basic structure is laid out for me and I don't need to reinvent the wheel every time I have a project. This saves me copious amounts of time. Even with all these tools, my secret to successfully writing with dictation is tenacity. You can have the best equipment, software and organizational skills. However, if you don't plant your butt in front of a microphone and talk, the words won't magically appear. Trust me, I wish I could just think about stories and have them show up for me to publish. Unfortunately, it doesn't work that way.

If I could go back and start my career over again with the knowledge I have now, one of the first things I would do is create a comprehensive story bible. When you write your first book, it's easy to think you'll never forget any detail about your characters because, after all, they are your babies.

I'm here to tell you – more than thirty books later – you *will* forget important details about your characters. So, if you are just starting, I recommend that you create a story Bible with crucial information about your characters. These can include physical traits, relationships, and personality quirks. It's easy to start when you have just a few characters, but as they begin to multiply, the idea of creating a story bible retroactively is daunting. I hope you can learn from my mistake.

 Don't forget to create a story bible to keep track of your characters. It's easier to start this process early. Creating one after the fact is a challenge.

Find yourself a mentor. The indie community is full of very successful authors. Watch what they do and try to apply their methods to the way you write. I owe my writing career to Linda Kage. She took the time to mentor and encourage me. I will forever be grateful. I spend a lot of time paying that kindness forward.

The last thing I'm going to say about success is that sometimes things happen beyond your control. For me, most often, those stumbling blocks revolve around my health. Sometimes things won't happen the way you planned. Part of being a successful writer is picking yourself up and brushing yourself off. Trying again can be one of the hardest things you'll ever do. If your dictating is interrupted by life, there's always another opportunity to improve. When the crisis ends, you can start again.

I hope you enjoyed this overview of dictation software, computer equipment and tools for authors. Ideally it will encourage you to try a new tool or become better at using dictation. Regardless of your writing style, dictation can be a powerful tool in your arsenal. I look forward to hearing from you about how dictation changed your workflow.

If you are interested in learning how to use Scrivener or how to use it more effectively, the next books in this series are perfect for you. _An Everyday Guide to Scrivener 3 for Mac_ and _An Everyday Guide to Scrivener 3 for Windows_ will be available soon. These guides will help you become familiar with the program and become comfortable – even if you are not a computer programmer.

Acknowledgements

I have lots of people to thank for this project. First, I would like to thank my fans for the feedback they gave me regarding *The Power of Dictation*. That feedback was the impetus for this book.

Kathy McGee, you have been nothing but heroic during this process. Not only do you make my work beautiful, you encourage me when tasks seem impossible. You were my number one cheerleader from the first word of this book to the last. Thank you so much for your help.

To my editor, Lisa Lee, you work hard to make sense of my ramblings. I appreciate the fact that you are willing to step out of your comfort zone to make my work better.

To Craig Martelle and the gang at 20Booksto50K®, thank you so much for giving me a platform to share my knowledge with other authors. Your continued support means the world.

A special shout out to my beta readers for catching the typos and inconsistent information which escape my notice. You help make me a better author. I owe a debt of gratitude to the people who helped me evaluate software.

Thank you to the teams at Nuance® and Krisp for answering my persistently awkward questions and giving me permission to use your product and names in my books.

I would be remiss if I didn't thank my number one cheerleaders, my husband, Leonard, and my son, Justin. They have graciously learned to enter a room quietly and wait for me to turn my microphone off and they don't even look at me funny when I talk to my computer for hours at a time. Without their help and support, I wouldn't be able to do what I do. I love you both.

Resources

Retailers and Equipment:

Nuance® (Nuance.com) – the software company which develops and supports Dragon® Dictate, Dragon® NaturallySpeaking, and Dragon® Anywhere.

KnowBrainer (Knowbrainer.com) – a software and adaptive equipment online retailer with comprehensive resources and an active forum and helpful equipment guides.

Andrea Electronics Mic

https://www.amazon.com/Andrea-Electronics-Canceling-Microphone-C1-1022400-1/dp/B004K371TQ

Blue Mic (https://www.bluedesigns.com) – The manufacturer of Yeti, Snowball, Raspberry microphones (among others). These are among the best microphones I've ever used for voice recognition software.

TalkTech (https://talktech.com/) – This company provides a privacy mask for dictating in public. Although initially developed for court reporters, they have products available for voice recognition users too.

Krisp (https://krisp.ai/) – This program creates a virtual microphone which screens out and necessary background noise.

Internet Communities:
Dragon Riders
(https://www.facebook.com/groups/1648134245
442422) – This forum, which covers both
versions of Dragon Professional Individual is
the most active group on Facebook. There are
many participants who are well-versed in both
programs and generous with their advice.
Dragon® NaturallySpeaking Users
(https://www.facebook.com/groups/dragonusers/
) – This group is also a Facebook group, but it's
focus tends to be tailored toward
NaturallySpeaking.

Sprinting Groups and Other Resources:
Grotto Garden
(https://www.facebook.com/groups/GrottoGarde
n/) – Need a sprinting partner any time, day or
night? Not a problem with this friendly group
of folks. Just hop on and introduce yourself.
The group is large enough that there are
usually sprints happening around the clock.
Sprinting with Friends
(https://www.facebook.com/groups/7733693494
01931/) – Is Facebook too much of a
temptation? This sprinting group might be for
you. The sprints actually take place in a Chatzy
group. It is a great group for keeping you on
task and accountable.
NaNoWriMo (http://nanowrimo.org/) – Why not
join us for National Novel Writing Month? Not

only is it a fun challenge, you'll meet lots of other great writers and find a website chock full of great writing tips and prompts. It's also a great way to practice sprinting and find discounts on software and editing programs.

My Write Club (http://www.mywriteclub.com) – This is a great little motivating sprinting site. I love this site because it is so flexible. You can join a group sprint which is a group of random people. They have twenty-five minute sprints at the top and bottom of every hour. You can race against a group of people. You earn stars along the way for your progress which is incredibly motivating. You can also set up your own private sprint by yourself or with a group of friends. You can track your progress toward your goal.

The Creative Penn (https://www.thecreativepenn.com/tag/dictation/) – Joanna Penn has a phenomenal site with great resources for authors. She has a page dedicated to dictation.

Software and Books:

Speech Productivity (http://www.speechproductivity.eu/) – This $25 to $45 add-in program for Dragon® Professional Individual for Windows is everything Dragon® Pad should be but isn't. I'm a huge fan.

Literature and Latte (https://www.literatureandlatte.com/) – Scrivener is their signature program (although they do make Scrapple). It is my go-to writing program. I own three versions of it.

Grammarly (Grammarly.com) – A web-based grammar checking program. They offer both free and paid versions. Aside from Scrivener, this is my favorite place to dictate.

ProWritingAid (https://prowritingaid.com) – a fee-based grammar checking program. You can buy a lifetime subscription. This program is particularly good at picking up homonyms and other errors created by using voice recognition software.

Vellum (https://vellum.pub/) – Vellum is formatting software for the Mac.

Novlr (https://novlr.org/) – A simple writing app designed by authors to encourage people to write in a distraction free environment while being able to add structure in detail to their work.

Dabble (https://www.dabblewriter.com/) – Another writing app designed to provide structure and a distraction free work environment.

StoryShop (https://storyshop.io) – A writing app which concentrates on world building and plot structure. It has character sheets to help flush out your characters.

Tomato One (https://apps.apple.com/us/app/tomato-one-free-focus-timer) – A flexible Pomodoro timer which allows you to set the amount of time you would like to write and the length of time you rest. It tracks the number of Pomodoro sessions you have completed each day.

Focus (Heyfocus.com) – a web blocking app for the Mac. which allows you to use Pomodoro timers and customize the websites you block.

Focus Me (https://focusme.com/) Focus me is an app designed to block websites and increase your productivity. It is available for both Windows and Mac.

Pacemaker Press (https://www.pacemaker.press) – One of the ways I stay motivated is to track my progress. My favorite way to do this is with Pacemaker Press. I can track multiple projects and plan out my year.

The Writer's Guide to Training Your Dragon®: Using Speech Recognition Software to Dictate Your Book and Supercharge Your Writing Workflow by Scott Baker (https://scottbakerbooks.com/books/) – a comprehensive guide to both Dragon® NaturallySpeaking and Dragon® Dictate. He includes information on using Parallels or Boot Camp to run Dragon® NaturallySpeaking on a Mac

Fool Proof Dictation: A No-Nonsense System for Effective & Rewarding Dictation by Christopher Downing (https://www.amazon.com/dp/B074M5C3SJ) – a series of comprehensive exercises to build up your skills and confidence to help you become an expert at dictation.

Dragon® Professional Individual For Dummies by Stephanie Diamond (https://www.amazon.com/Dragon-Professional-Individual-Dummies-Computer-ebook-dp-B019HRL4U6/dp/B019HRL4U6) – this is the single most comprehensive guide to Dragon® Professional Individual for Windows I've run across. It covers the material in much more depth, including some more information on commands and scripting.

The 8-Minute Writing Habit for Novelists: Triple Your Writing Speed and Learn Dictation to Produce More Words,Faster by Monica Leonelle (https://theworldneedsyourbook.com/dictationresouces) – This book incorporates dictation into an overall strategy of writing faster. Dictation is just one component of a mindset of increasing your productivity.

On Being a Dictator: Using Dictation to Be a Better Writer by Kevin J. Anderson and Martin L. Shoemaker (https://www.amazon.com/gp/product/B07TY JLJNS/) – Although I strongly disagree with the premise that it is okay to dictate while you drive, this book has some solid tips for using transcription – Including equipment recommendations.

About the Author

I have been lucky enough to live my own version of a romance novel. I married the guy who kissed me at summer camp. He told me on the night we met that he was going to marry me and be the father of my children.

Eventually, I stopped giggling when he said it, and we've been married for more than thirty years. We have two children. The oldest is a Doctor of Osteopathy. He is across the United States completing his residency, but when he's done, he is going to come back to Oregon and practice Family Medicine. Our youngest son is now tackling high school, where he is an honor student. He is interested in becoming an EMT.

I write full time now. I have published more than thirty books and have several more underway. I volunteer my time to a variety of causes. I have worked as a Civil Rights Attorney and Diversity Advocate. I spent several years working for various social service agencies before becoming an attorney.

In my spare time, I love to cook, decorate cakes and, of course, I obsessively, compulsively read.

I would be honored if you would take a few moments out of your busy day to check out my website, MaryCrawfordAuthor.com. While you're there, you can sign up for my newsletter and get a free book. I will be announcing my upcoming books and giving sneak peeks as well as sponsoring giveaways and giving you information about other interesting events.

If you have questions or comments, please E-mail me at Mary@MaryCrawfordAuthor.com or find me on the following social networks:

Facebook:
www.facebook.com/authormarycrawford

Website:
MaryCrawfordAuthor.com

Twitter:
www.twitter.com/MaryCrawfordAut

Books by Mary Crawford

Hidden Beauty Series

Until the Stars Fall from the Sky
So the Heart Can Dance
Joy and Tiers
Love Naturally
Love Seasoned
Love Claimed
If You Knew Me (and other silent musings) (novella)
Jude's Song
The Price of Freedom (novella)
Paths Not Taken
Dreams Change (novella)
Heart Wish (100% charity release)
Tempting Fate
The Letter
The Power of Will

Hidden Hearts Series

Identity of the Heart
Sheltered Hearts
Hearts of Jade
Port in the Storm (novella)
Love is More Than Skin Deep
Tough
Rectify
Pieces (a crossover novel)

Hearts Set Free
Freedom (a crossover novel)
The Long Road to Love (novella)

Hidden Hearts – Protection Unit

Love and Injustice
Out of Thin Air
Soul Scars

Other Works

The Power of Dictation
Use Your Voice
An Everyday Guide to Scrivener 3 for Mac (**Coming Soon**)
An Everyday Guide to Scrivener 3 for Windows (**Coming Soon**)
Vision of the Heart
#AmWriting: A Collection of Letters to Benefit The Wayne Foundation

Index

The Power of Dictation
Pro Tips for Authors: Make Dragon® Work for You

Wish your words could magically appear?

You are not alone.

What if I told you your wish is within reach? Dictation isn't magic, but it can seem like it. However, it can be daunting, overwhelming, and downright confusing. I've been using voice recognition software for thirty years and written over thirty books using both Dragon® Dictate for Mac and various versions of Dragon® NaturallySpeaking. n this updated and expanded version of *The Power of Dictation*, I demystify the world of voice recognition software for you.

- Learn how to choose the right computer, microphone, and software for your needs.
- This book covers the latest releases from Nuance, including Dragon® Professional Individual for Mac 6.0.8 (Dragon® Dictate) and Dragon® Professional Individual 15.3 for Windows (Dragon® NaturallySpeaking), and discusses how they stack up against other alternatives.

- If you are a Mac user, learn how to get the most out of Dragon® Dictate without having to use an alternative operating system on your Mac.
- Explore positive ways to make the transition from using your keyboard to using your voice to tell stories. • Discover how to increase your efficiency and productivity as you dictate.
- Learn how to take your dictation mobile through the use of transcription.

Unlock the power of dictation and take your writing to a whole new level.

For more information visit:
http://marycrawfordauthor.com/project/the-power-of-dictation/

Empowering Productivity
Series

(Available in eBook & Paperback)

http://marycrawfordauthor.com/project/the-power-of-dictation/

http://marycrawfordauthor.com/project/use-your-voice/

ॐ

An Everyday Guide to Scrivener 3 for Mac and *An Everyday Guide to Scrivener 3* for Windows will be available soon. These guides will help you become familiar with the program and become comfortable – even if you are not a computer programmer.

https://marycrawfordauthor.com/project/an-everyday-guide-to-scrivener-3-for-mac/

https://marycrawfordauthor.com/project/an-everyday-guide-to-scrivener-3-for-windows/